Differentiating Instruction

in a Whole-Group Setting

Differentiating Instruction
in a Whole-Group Setting

Taking the Easy
FIRST STEPS
into Differentiation

by Betty Hollas

Crystal Springs
BOOKS

A division of 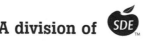 Staff Development for Educators

Peterborough, New Hampshire

Published by Crystal Springs Books
A division of Staff Development for Educators (SDE)
10 Sharon Road
P.O. Box 500
Peterborough, NH 03458
1-800-321-0401
www.crystalsprings.com
www.sde.com

© 2005 Crystal Springs Books
Published 2005
Printed in the United States of America
09 08 07 06 05   1 2 3 4 5

ISBN 1-884548-70-9

Library of Congress Cataloging-in-Publication Data

Hollas, Betty, 1948–
    Differentiating instruction in a whole-group setting : taking the easy
first steps into differentiation/ by Betty Hollas.
        p.   cm.
    Includes index.
    ISBN 1-884548-70-9
    1. Individualized instruction. 2. Lesson planning. I. Title.
    LB1031.H63 2005
    371.39'4—dc22

                                                            2004026654

Editor: Sharon Smith
Art director, designer, and production coordinator: Coni Porter
Illustrator: Cheryl Wolf

To my husband, Dave,
for always encouraging and supporting me
through the chapters of my life.

Contents

ACKNOWLEDGMENTS

Thank you to:

Sharon Smith, a talented editor, with whom it is an honor and a joy to work.

Coni Porter, designer, art director, and production coordinator, who is responsible for making me look good.

Cheryl Wolf, the artist who supplied the visuals that enhance this book.

Lorraine Walker, Staff Development for Educators Vice President of Publishing and New Product Development, who had the idea for this book.

Deb Fredericks, Publishing Coordinator at S.D.E., for keeping everything on schedule.

Jim Grant, Executive Director of Staff Development for Educators, speaker, author and friend, and to Char Forsten, Associate Executive Director of Staff Development for Educators, speaker, author, and friend—both of whom are an endless source of ideas, inspiration, and good times.

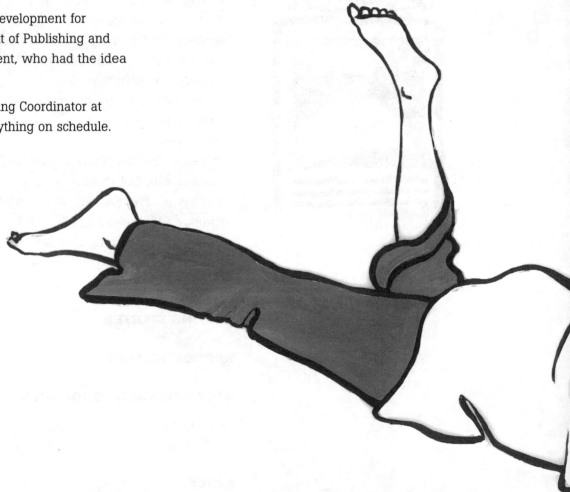

Introduction

oes the title of this book sound a little strange to you? I think the official word for it would be *oxymoron*. How could you possibly differentiate instruction in a whole-group setting? You're probably thinking that this author must be nuts! Actually, I often am nuts, as well as sort of wild and crazy. But this time, I really do want to give you something to think about.

Do you know the story about the famous educator who was talking with the famous neurosurgeon? The educator said that the decisions teachers make are more important and more difficult than the decisions made in any other profession. The story goes that the neurosurgeon wasn't so sure about that. "How can you say that the decisions a

teacher makes are more important and more difficult than decisions made in any other profession?" he wanted to know. "Look at me. I operate on the brain. I've got life and death right there on the table in front of me."

The famous educator responded, "Yes, sir, but you operate on one patient at a time, and that patient is anesthetized!"

In today's classrooms, your job might be easier if you were like the neurosurgeon and could deal with one "patient" at a time. But we're talking about real life. It's much more likely that you teach students who learn at different rates, who have a wide range of abilities and experiences, and who challenge you at every step of the way. Am I right? It's probably becoming more and more difficult for you to meet the needs of all of your students. It's certainly becoming more and more important. If you're going to meet your state's standards for the wide range of students in your classroom, you're going to need to find ways to adapt your instruction to meet the individual needs of each student.

Does that sound pretty overwhelming? Does it conjure up visions of an individual lesson plan for every student, a school day filled with small groups that are constantly changing, and lots of centers or stations set up in the classroom? Does it also conjure up images of you staying up all night, trying to figure out how to make it all happen?

I'm sure that you want to do a good job and be successful, and I know that you already have plenty of demands on your time. (I have never once had a teacher tell

QUESTIONING: alternatives to the passive, answer-giving, fact-finding style of whole-group instruction—the one in which the question most often asked is: "Does everyone understand?"

STUDENT ENGAGEMENT: alternatives to the "sit-and-git," "my-way-or-the-highway," "chalk-and-talk," and "spray-and-pray" approaches to whole-group instruction

me, "I just wish my administrator would give me more to do during the day!") So this is the point when your instinct might be to throw up your hands and say to yourself, "This too shall pass . . . I've been in this business long enough . . . the pendulum swings. . . ." and so on. Then you'd be tempted to shut the door and just continue teaching in the way you're most comfortable—in a whole-group setting.

Relax. You can do that and still differentiate.

You're focusing on the standards your students are expected to meet. You're worrying about how you can possibly address every student's needs and still meet those standards. You have a right to be concerned. But you also need to recognize your own abilities to differentiate instruction in ways that really will help all your students to be successful.

And you need to know that you can do this while you are teaching the whole group.

In fact, you may discover that you're already differentiating. You just didn't know it. And you may not have known how much more you could do with differentiation even within the whole-group setting.

WHAT IS DIFFERENTIATED INSTRUCTION ANYWAY?

In its simplest form, differentiated instruction means that you are consistently and proactively creating different pathways to help all your students to be successful. For example, when you give your students a choice of reading materials related to a common theme, you are differentiating your instruction according to what the students are interested in reading. This is different from having everyone in the class read the same book that you've chosen. It's perhaps easier to use just one book, but that's not necessarily the ideal pathway for every student. Make sense? You're probably already thinking of some kind of differentiation you do right now that is proactive and that

FLEXIBLE GROUPING: alternatives to the room arrangement preferred by your school's overburdened custodian—the one in which students sit in rows, passively staring at you while fake listening or fake reading for much of the day

ONGOING ASSESSMENT: alternatives to the teach-teach-teach-then-assess approach to whole-group instruction

helps all your students to be successful.

You see, differentiating instruction in a whole-group setting doesn't have to add to the burdens in your classroom. Rather, it can bring fun and excitement to learning, and it can make you a better teacher. You'll be helping all your students to succeed. That's the goal of differentiation. That's the goal of standards. And I bet that's your goal as a teacher, too.

WINDOWS OF OPPORTUNITY

What differentiated instruction does is to open up more options for more students, so that everybody has a chance to succeed. I like to think of it in terms of windows of opportunity, because that's what differentiated instruction really is—a bunch of opportunities to help every one of your students to succeed. In this book, I'm going to describe four of those windows and explain how you can open them for your students.

These are the four windows: student engagement, questioning, flexible grouping, and ongoing assessment.

I'm devoting one chapter to each of these "windows." Each chapter begins with a look at the opportunity itself, and then continues with lots of strategies to use in your classroom. Within each strategy you'll find:

- An overview of the strategy
- The steps or choices involved in using the strategy in your classroom
- A quick look back to see just how this strategy fits into the concept of differentiated instruction

Differentiating instruction in your classroom doesn't have to be an overwhelming thing. It really doesn't. Yes, it adds a certain complexity to teaching. But it's manageable. You can do this. And this book will show you how.

Now, turn the page and say aloud (yes, aloud): "Let's get going!"

Chapter 1

Student Engagement Window

In baseball, the pitcher is the most powerful player, the one who controls the game. Nothing can happen until the pitcher throws the baseball. The pitcher determines what pitches to throw, and he determines the speed and location of the ball. The greater the variety of pitches a pitcher can throw, the more he can influence the success of his team. The better the pitcher knows the kind of hitter he faces, the better he can direct his pitches to influence what the batter does at the plate.

Like the pitcher in baseball, the classroom teacher who has the most control and the greatest number of options is the one who has the greatest chance of succeeding. Like the pitcher in baseball, the better you know each person you're "pitching" to, the better you can pick strategies that help certain students to be more successful while keeping all students active and engaged. And student engagement is a great window of opportunity for differentiating instruction.

Sometimes in whole-group instruction, it's tempting to rely on old habits of "sit and git" with a heavy emphasis on lectures, videos, quizzes, and reading from the textbook. But think about this for a minute. You know those days when your students start getting up out of their seats and taking those "in-class field trips"? The times when they start talking to their neighbors, or looking at their watches? (My favorite is the kid who looks at his watch—and then hits the watch with his other hand to make sure it's working!) Sometimes those are the days you resort to the "my-way-or-the-highway" approach. Those are the times you wonder whether there really is a nurturing way to tell students that you have one nerve left and they're getting on it!

What's happened, of course, is that you've totally lost control of the class, and possibly you've lost control of yourself, too. Remember that baseball pitcher? When he loses control, it's no big deal. That's when the manager sends in a relief pitcher. Wouldn't that be nice, if a "relief teacher" could step in for you? As teachers, we don't get that option. Instead, the days when you lose control are the days you begin to get negative. That may be the time you go to the teachers' lounge and get in a good session with the "B.M.W. Club." Do you know that club? "B.M.W." stands for "bitch, moan, and whine." You become a member in good standing if you spend most of that time in the teachers' lounge complaining to your colleagues about how this is the most unmotivated class you've ever had.

I'd like to show you another way to look at things. When teaching relies almost entirely on the "sit-and-git" approach, and your students start acting up, they're just playing out their part of the ritual. Their part is minimal involvement, minimal motivation, and minimal compliance with the rules in their classroom.

But you have the power to change your students' behavior.

In this chapter you'll find easy-to-implement strategies that will keep students active and engaged in learning. You'll also discover how you can use these strategies to differentiate instruction for many of the students you teach.

A DIFFERENT KIND OF CONTROL

In baseball, the pitcher doesn't get control of the game by constantly exercising his authority; he doesn't rely on hitting batters or on walking everyone who steps up to the plate. By the same token, you control your classroom not so much by exercising your authority as by making the effort to know each student. Differentiating instruction begins with knowing not only the material you teach but also the student you're teaching. By that I mean that you need to know certain things about each student in your class. Those things include:

- The child's readiness to handle the content you're teaching
- The child's interests
- How the child learns best
- How the child feels about the classroom, about himself, and about learning

And that's not all! In addition to knowing your individual students, you gain control in your classroom through:

- The relationships you build with your students
- The pathways you open for them to construct meaning from the content you teach
- The ways you structure students' interaction with one another
- How you encourage children to interact with the information they are learning in ways that challenge them, engage them, and keep them actively involved.

WHAT DOES THIS HAVE TO DO WITH DIFFERENTIATING INSTRUCTION ANYWAY?

Students are engaged and are actively learning when students are doing. In other words, students are learning when they're the ones doing most of the work. Children need to actively solve problems, question, and apply what they're learning, because when they do those things, they're making meaning and manipulating content.

Often, students who are engaged in the learning process will be out of their seats and moving about the classroom. Wasn't that exactly what the B.M.W. Club was complaining about? Sure it is. But when you're differentiating your teaching, you actually *want* those kids to be out of their seats—because you know that's a great way to get kids thinking. The difference is that they'll be out of their seats legitimately!

Brain research suggests that there is a definite link between learning and movement (*Teaching with the Brain in Mind*, Jensen 1998). Students are engaged when they are actively involved in classroom conversations and discussing information with others. They retain more when they have an opportunity to discuss information as it's presented. In other words, when students are interacting with others, their brains are more engaged.

And you can open the window even wider. When you lecture, you're addressing the auditory learners in your class. (Watch out, though: if the lecture goes on and on, even those auditory learners will begin to "fake listen" about 60% of the time.) When you add pictures, charts, graphs, etc. to a lesson, you are appealing to the visual learners. You're also increasing retention (i.e., the length of time the average child retains the information) by as much as 38% for the majority of your students (Pike, 1989). When you add direct student involvement in a lesson and "hands-on" manipulation of information, you include the kinesthetic learners in your room as well. So now, instead of reaching one very narrow segment of your class, you've found a way to get everyone involved. And you're still working at the whole-group level.

WHAT'S YOUR TEACHING STYLE?

Because of the many advances in cognitive science in recent years, we now have a much better understanding of how students learn. But sometimes what we understand is one thing and what we instinctively *do* is something entirely different. (Have you ever had the experience of buying an exercise bike and setting great goals for using it because you knew it would be good for your health? And have you ever ended up using the thing just as a clothes rack? If you have, then you know exactly what I'm talking about.)

If you've been teaching for a while, you may well have been taught in traditional ways. You probably went to class, sat in a row of desks, and stared at the big person in the front of the room—the one who did almost all of the talking. Your natural tendency is to teach the way you were taught, and so you instinctively repeat that pattern.

Most of us also tend to teach in the way that we ourselves learn. That means that if you are a verbal/linguistic kind of person, you may lean toward lecturing. If your strength is in computers and visuals, you may have a dyna-

> **HOLD THIS THOUGHT**
> I want you to remember one thing above all as you look at the strategies in this chapter: The more ways you teach, the more students you will reach!

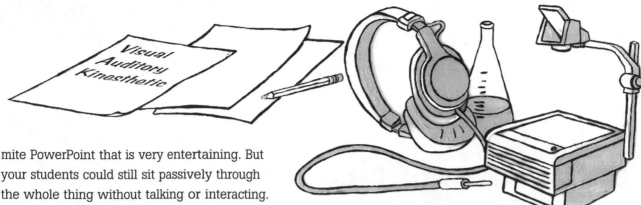

mite PowerPoint that is very entertaining. But your students could still sit passively through the whole thing without talking or interacting.

If you are a very social, interpersonal kind of person, you may lean heavily on talking, organizing, and going full-steam through the material you have to get through between September and June. In fact, you may focus so strongly on getting through the material that you don't give enough attention to having students reflect on and process what they're learning.

The challenge in a whole-group setting of diverse learners is to avoid teaching solely in the way you were taught or the way you learn best. If you teach the way you were taught or the way you learn best, then you're unconsciously overlooking the needs of many of your students, the ones whose learning styles happen to be different from yours. Your students will be more successful if you can objectively think about your teaching style— and then go beyond your own comfort zone to meet the wide range of learners in your class.

Think about it for a minute. If you took the time and energy to write down individual students' learning styles, interests, and so on, would you really be addressing the fact that your students differ? Would you be saying that you're going to do whatever it takes to engage the whole range of learners with the content you're teaching? Sure you would!

You're truly differentiating instruction in the student engagement window when you include a variety of multisensory approaches in your instruction. But you can do even better than that. As a good teacher, you know your individual students' abilities, interests,

skills, and learning styles. You may not consciously think about it, and you may not have written it down, but I bet you know all of those things. The question is: what do you do with what you know?

Suppose you had a student in your class who was a strong auditory learner. Would you be willing to read (or find a volunteer to read) written work into a tape recorder so the student could play it back? If you felt it would truly help that student, I bet you would.

This is very different from being the "sage on the stage" and pouring your knowledge into your students. It means getting away from just covering your curriculum in the single best way you know and hoping most of the students get it.

Differentiated instruction means recognizing that learning is not a spectator sport.

IN OTHER WORDS

With all of these thoughts in mind, the strategies in this chapter promote student engagement by emphasizing:

- Movement
- Interaction with others
- Interaction with the content

You cannot just pour information into the MTV-, multimedia-bombarded brains of your students today. Student engagement is the only way to go!

Now, with all that as background, let's get going!

Appointment Calendar

he appointment calendar is a great way to pair off students for any activity or discussion.

STEP BY STEP

• Make one copy of the Daily Appointment Calendar reproducible on page 96 for each student in your class.

• Give each student a copy.

• Have students stand up, take their appointment calendars, and find other students with whom to make appointments. Explain that each time a child makes an appointment, he should enter the appropriate name in his appointment book next to the agreed-upon time. The calendars must agree. If Ed is Matt's 10:00 appointment, then Matt must be Ed's 10:00 appointment.

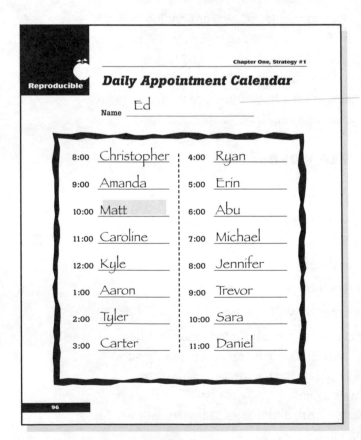

- Students are responsible for keeping up with their daily calendars once the calendars are filled in.

- You now have a way to pair students. This comes in handy when you want kids from different groups to be moving and interacting with each other. For example, in English/language arts, you might say, "Each of you please get out your appointment calendar and meet with your 2:00 appointment. The two of you should discuss how the novel you are currently reading depicts the era in which it was written." Or in science, you might say, "Please meet with your 4:00 appointment and discuss how humans cause chemical and physical weathering."

- When you look at the reproducible for the appointment book, you'll notice that times are listed all the way up to 11 o'clock at night. Don't worry. It's not that differentiating means you'll have to extend the school day until 11 PM! The times in the appointment books are just a way of identifying who's paired with whom for a particular activity. It may be 10 o'clock in the morning when you ask children to meet with their 9 PM appointments.

- Want to build on this strategy? If you ask each student to walk at least seven steps to find a partner, that extra bit of exercise will get more oxygen to that child's brain. And that can help get rid of those mental cobwebs.

- To make the curriculum even more accessible in this case, you may want to strategically select a few of the partners yourself. For example, you might be the one who identifies the 12 o'clock partners in the room. You might arrange for

good readers to be paired with weaker readers, and have the students read the same piece of text to each other. The better reader would go first to provide modeling and support; then the weaker reader would take his turn.

VARIATION

Instead of pairing weaker and stronger readers, you can arrange, say, the 9 o'clock appointments to pair off students who are at the same reading level. Only you will know how you strategically selected the pairings. You can then make sure each pair is reading materials at the appropriate level of difficulty.

NOW LOOK WHAT YOU'VE DONE!

You've differentiated for a specific learning modality. This strategy is great for those bodily/kinesthetic learners, and that's a help for them *and* you. If you don't give those kids legitimate ways to move, they'll find their own ways—and you may not be so happy with the times they pick! This approach gives them a purpose for moving around.

MAKING THE CURRICULUM ACCESSIBLE

If you're going to differentiate instruction, then you must be constantly aware of the instructional needs of each student so that you can make the curriculum accessible to all students.

What do I mean by "making the curriculum accessible to all students"? Well, for a long time, we thought in terms of "modifying the curriculum." I personally like to use the phrase "making the curriculum accessible to all students." To me, that implies the intent of differentiating your instruction: to create a variety of pathways to learning, so that every student has an opportunity to be successful. The change in language reflects a new way of thinking about our students.

Timed-Pair Paraphrase

Instead of just asking students to think about a topic and share their thoughts, go one step further and time each student's sharing. This approach is adapted from a couple of cooperative learning structures (Kagan, 1994, 1998). It's a simple strategy that can make a big difference.

STEP BY STEP

- Ask students to refer to their appointment calendars (see pages 8–9) and meet with one of their appointment partners. (Tell them to meet with their 1 o'clock appointment partners, for example.)

- When students have found their partners, say, "Decide which of you has the biggest foot. I want Big Foot to tell Little Foot how the novel you're reading depicts the era in which it was written. You have two minutes. Little Foot, if your partner quits sharing, ask questions."

- Set a timer. After two (or any number) of minutes, ask Little Foot to thank Big Foot for sharing and to tell Big Foot what he remembers that Big Foot said. The paraphrase might start, "I heard you say..." (This will improve those listening skills!)

- Ask several Little Feet to share with the class what their partners said.

- Reverse the process so that each Little Foot can share.

NOW LOOK WHAT YOU'VE DONE!

There's a specific reason you are structuring the sharing by timing each student. You know you have those "hogs" and "logs" in your classroom. If you just ask the students to engage in a discussion, the hog will talk the entire time and the log will check out and think about what's for lunch. A Timed-Pair Paraphrase lets you control that.

By using this strategy, you're helping the log to be successful because you're inviting her into the discussion. You're also differentiating, because part of differentiating is knowing each student and then opening a pathway to success for that student. See? I told you you could do this!

Carousel Your Way Through a K-W-L

What do you do when you try to use a K-W-L (What I Know, What I Want to Know, What I Learned) strategy with your class and it just flops? Maybe you ask your students, "What do you know about rocks and minerals?" and they say, "Nothing." You say, "What would you like to know?" and they say, "Nothing." You think, "This is the most unmotivated group I've ever had!" and then you go to the B.M.W. Club (remember the Bitch, Moan, and Whine Club?) during your next break.

Part of making a commitment to differentiating instruction is making a commitment to being a responsive teacher. Instead of blaming the students, ask yourself what you could do to make the K-W-L strategy a little more interactive.

One way is to turn it into a carousel.

STEP BY STEP

- Decide on the major topics students will cover during a particular unit and write each of those topics on a sheet of chart paper; then post each sheet of chart paper in a different area of the classroom. If students are studying the settling of the West, you might post three charts: one headed "Ways of Living," one headed "Food," and one headed "Location."

- Divide students into the same number of groups as there are charts hanging in the room (in this example, three).

- Give each group a marker in a different color, and ask those students to go to one of the charts.

- Ask each group to appoint a recorder. The recorder's job is to list on the chart the things the group thinks they know about the topic.

- After a few minutes, have them rotate to another chart. Ask each group to review what the other students already wrote on that chart, put a checkmark (with the marker that's their color) beside those things they also knew about the topic, and then make their own additions to the list.

- Tell the students that at this point they should just ignore anything they think is wrong. As they read and study the material, it will become clearer whether anything needs to be changed.

- Keep this up until all students are back at the charts they started with. Now ask each group to select a reporter.

- Give everyone a few minutes to look over all the information now on their charts. Then ask each reporter to give the class a brief verbal summary of the information on the chart her group started.

- After each group reports, ask the class to think of some questions they have about each of the topics. List these in writing on the board so that all the students can see and refer to them during their study.

- After they complete the unit of study, have students return to the charts and discuss what they've learned both within their original groups and with the entire class.

NOW LOOK WHAT YOU'VE DONE!

You've gotten students up and moving around, which helps the kinesthetic learners. You've got them talking and listening, which helps the auditory learners. And you've got them making lists, which helps the visual learners. Hey, you're differentiating!

FOR STUDENTS WHO ALREADY KNOW THE TOPIC

What if, during the carousel recording of "What We Know About the Topic," you observe several students who already seem to know even more than you do? You know the students I'm talking about—the ones who could easily sub for you when you're absent—and do a good job!

Try having those students opt out of some of the other activities associated with this unit and work on independent projects related to the unit of study. For example, ask each of those students to select a specific in-depth question the class has come up with, research that question, and then make a presentation to the class.

Vocabulary on the Move

For years I taught vocabulary only with dictionary definitions. My students were really good at looking up the words and writing the definitions five times. In fact they got so good they could even make up definitions that sounded as if they had really looked up the words. They could score 100% on vocabulary test day—as long as I gave them the test the very first thing on Friday morning before I even spoke to them!

Then on Monday, it was as if the words were in a foreign language.

Have you been there? Well, the good news is that we know a lot more about teaching vocabulary now. Vocabulary instruction, like most good teaching, needs student engagement—and that means a lot more than just looking up words in the dictionary. Here's one way to get those vocabulary words into your students' long-term memories.

STEP BY STEP

- Make a list of vocabulary terms your students have been learning. These should be terms students are familiar with; they can include words from previous units. Write the terms on sentence strips. Then staple the ends of each strip together to make a headband.

- Ask each student to put on a headband without looking at the word on that headband.

- Create a list of questions on the board. Tell students that each child's goal is to guess the word on her headband. Explain that students can figure out their words by walking around the room and asking other students questions from the list on the board. Tell students to leave their headbands on even if they think they know their words.

- After a few minutes of playing the game, ask those students who think they know their words to tell the class what they've figured out and why they think they're right.

- Once they've done that, ask all students to remove their headbands. Celebrate with all students the experience of try- ing to figure out their words. Let those who came up with their words—as well as those who didn't—talk about some of the questions they asked about their words, answers they were given, etc.

NOW LOOK WHAT YOU'VE DONE!

This kind of active involvement is a key component of differentiated instruction. By getting your students actively engaged in learning, you've greatly increased the likeli- hood that they'll retain what they've learned.

Show—Don't Tell

One of the best ways for students to learn vocabulary is to associate each new word with a visual or with movement. All of your students will get into this student-centered vocabulary strategy, but it's especially good for all those visual/spatial and bodily/kinesthetic learners.

STEP BY STEP

- Give each student a list that shows the vocabulary words the class is studying and the definitions for those words.

- Give each student an index card with one of the words on it, plus a large piece of paper and a bunch of markers in assorted colors.

- Tell the class that each student should draw a picture of her word and then figure out a way to act out that word. Explain that each child needs to do this without showing other students the word on her card.

- Have each student come to the front of the room, show the class his picture, and act out his word. For example, let's say you give a student a card with the word "collaborate," and the list of definitions says that "collaborate" means "to work jointly together." A student might draw puzzle pieces fitting together, and his action might be shaking hands.

- Ask the other students to guess the word. Once they've figured it out, have all the students repeat the action.

- Each time a student comes to the front and acts out a word, follow up by leading the class in a review of all the words presented so far. To do this, have the class say each word and act out the motion.

- At the end of the session, collect all the pictures.

- The next day, for a quick review, show each picture and have students act out the word associated with that picture.

NOW LOOK WHAT YOU'VE DONE!

By offering your students multiple pathways to success, you've opened up the learning process to a much wider range of learners. And that means you've given your students a much greater chance of working those vocabulary words into long-term memory.

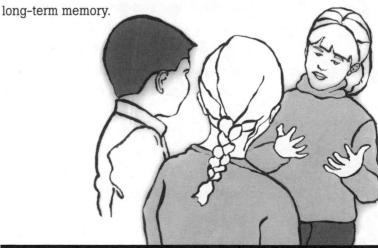

Snowball Fight

This activity involves movement and engages students. It can be used for review, predicting, summarizing learning, and more. And if you live in the South, like me, this may be the closest you and some of your students ever get to seeing snow!

STEP BY STEP

- Let's say you'd like students to reflect on the day's course content. Ask each student to put his name on a piece of paper and then to write on that paper something learned in class that day.

- Have students bring their papers and form a large circle.

- Tell students that each child should wad her paper up into a ball. On your signal, they should all throw their papers into the center of the circle. Then each child should grab somebody else's "ball" from the pile and throw *it* into the center of the circle.

- Continue this "snowball fight" for as long as you can stand it (like about one minute). Then signal the students to stop.

- Have each student pick up any snowball that has landed close by.

- Call on a few students to read to the rest of the class the "snowballs" they've found. Be sure to comment on the "snowballs." For correct information you might say something like, "I can tell you were really

THE BUTTON PUSHER

What do you do about the student who writes, "I learned nothing"? That student is probably trying to "push your buttons," so you might just say, "Well, I bet tomorrow you'll learn something." Later you might reconnect with that student to discuss what the problem is.

listening today." For incorrect information, you might say something like, "Interesting thought. Let's discuss it a minute."

- Collect all snowballs for assessment purposes.

VARIATION

For a daily review, choose three to five topics from things the class is studying. Write one of these topics at the tops of several pieces of paper, then do the same with each of the other topics. Wad up the pieces of paper and toss them on the floor. Have each student grab a snowball and open it up, then write on the paper his name and something he learned about that topic. Toss the snowballs again and then repeat the process as above.

NOW LOOK WHAT YOU'VE DONE!

This is another aspect of differentiating: using ongoing assessment to drive your instruction. If a student gives an incorrect response—or no response at all—on the paper, that tells you this student needs some extra instruction. If he writes "Beats me!" that's a pretty good clue, too!

That's Me!

This strategy offers a great way to build community in your classroom and to get students acquainted with each other at the beginning of the school year. It also gets students moving, because you're asking them to do more than just raise their hands.

STEP BY STEP

- Explain to your students that you're going to make a statement such as:

  ✓ "I have a pet."

  ✓ "My favorite subject is math."

  ✓ "I have been in this school district since I was in kindergarten."

  ✓ "I like to watch TV on the weekends."

  ✓ "I hate homework."

- Tell students that when you make a statement, anyone for whom that statement is true should stand and say, "That's me!"

NOW LOOK WHAT YOU'VE DONE!

An important part of working together in a differentiated classroom is building a community of learners. When you structure activities that give students a chance to get to know one another, they get some insight into other students with whom they have things in common.

FOR LATER IN THE YEAR

Come back to this activity later in the year and give it a slight twist. This time, tell students that you'll be making statements related to topics they've been studying. Statements might be something like these:

- "I know two possible explanations for _____."

- "I know how _____ is related to _____."

- "I know two books by _____."

- "I can summarize _____."

This time, those students who know the answer should stand and say, "That's Me!" Then you can call on one or two students to give the answers.

Vote with Your Feet & Not Your Hands

The title of this strategy does not mean that your students stand on their hands to vote. Rather, they're going to move to one side of the classroom or another to agree or disagree with a statement. This strategy is guaranteed to energize and engage your students.

STEP BY STEP

- Make a statement such as, "Students should be required to wear uniforms to school."

- Tell students that they should move to one side of the room if they agree with the statement and to the opposite side if they disagree.

- Ask individual students to explain and elaborate upon their viewpoints. Be sure to accept all answers, and encourage a discussion.

NOW LOOK WHAT YOU'VE DONE!

In a differentiated classroom, you want students to be thinking and doing. When you ask them a question that has no single correct answer, the question becomes an invitation to think. You've engaged students' minds. If you ask them to get up out of their seats and stand on one side of the room to vote, you've got their bodies engaged as well. And the struggling learners in your class may get an added benefit, because sometimes hearing the thinking of others can help struggling learners to develop their own thought processes.

Abraham Lincoln was one of the best presidents

What's My Name?

Here's a fun, active way to do a quick review, get students up and moving, and reinforce learning.

STEP BY STEP

• Give each student a stick-on name tag, but don't write the student's name on it. Instead, use content from a unit of study. For example, give each student a name tag with a math fact written on it. The tag might say "8 x 8." Don't include the "64."

• Have students walk around the room learning the new "names" of their classmates. If Aaron's name tag is the one that says, "8 x 8," then Aaron's new name is "64." Have students call one another by their new names for as long as you think it's appropriate.

• This can also give you an opportunity to do some one-on-one teaching while everyone else is engaged in the activity. Let's say you know that Jimmy really doesn't know his math facts. You get in the game by wearing several name tags with those math facts that Jimmy doesn't know. You make sure that Jimmy has to call you by all your names. You also prompt him as necessary.

VARIATION

This works for other areas of the curriculum, too. In science, when the class is studying animal groups, Charlene's name tag might read "shrimp." That means her new name is "Arthropod."

NOW LOOK WHAT YOU'VE DONE!

You've engaged all your students and given them a chance to review content in a physically active way. At the same time, you've been able to give a little extra coaching to a student who needs it. Clever, huh? See? You can do this!

Circle the Category

This strategy helps students to develop vocabulary and to organize and categorize information. It can be used either before or after reading.

STEP BY STEP

- Give each student an index card.

- Ask each student to write on the card one word pertaining to a topic the class has studied or is about to study. If the class has been learning about rocks, a student might write "igneous" on the index card.

- Have students get up and move about the room comparing index cards. Then ask them to cluster into groups according to how they think words might go together. For example, students with "igneous," "sedimentary," and "metamorphic" on their index cards might decide to stand together.

- Once students have grouped themselves, give each group a large sheet of paper and a marker and ask them to write a label for their cluster of words. The igneous-sedimentary-metamorphic group might decide the label for their cluster is "Types of Rocks."

- Have one student hold the paper while the rest of the group makes a circle around her. Then ask each group to choose one member to explain to the rest of the class why the group clustered together and why they chose their particular label.

VARIATIONS

Variation 1: If students don't know enough about the topic to generate the words themselves, you can generate the words and write them on the index cards.

Variation 2: Show the class a picture from a chapter in a textbook they're about to read. Have them generate a list of words based on the picture. Assign each student one of the words from the list to write on an index card, then pick up the activity from there.

Variation 3: If you find that some students are already quite knowledgeable about a topic before the class begins that unit of study, you can build on this strategy. Have those students who already know a lot about the topic lead a class discussion about it. This allows those students to work on their speaking and presentation skills, and at the same time it helps those who don't know much about the topic to build their prior knowledge. Engaging in this strategy before reading helps all students better understand the content. Better yet, it encourages all students to see each other as sources of information.

• In some cases you might find that, before they study a particular topic, some of the students are unable to generate any words relating to that topic. On the other hand, some students may ask for more index cards. (If they ask for more cards, give 'em more cards!)

NOW LOOK WHAT YOU'VE DONE!

You've taught categorization, you've fostered higher level thinking, and—if you asked students to use this strategy before they read the material—you've gained an opportunity to find out what they knew or didn't know about the topic you were about to study.

Milling to Music

This is a quick and very flexible way to incorporate movement and student engagement in any lesson.

STEP BY STEP

- Tell students you're going to play some music (upbeat music works best) and that when the music starts, you want them to get up and mill about the classroom.

- Explain that when you stop the music, students are to freeze.

- When the music stops and the students freeze, ask them a question that requires a number as an answer. For example, you might say, "How many blind mice were there?"

- Have students quickly get in groups. Since the answer in this case was three, they'd get into groups of three. If some students are left over, tell them they are in the "lost and found" and ask them to join any group. On the next round, ask students to make sure those children are included in a group first.

- Now give students any content to discuss. They could discuss an author's use of a particular word in something the class has read. They could talk about methods for solving math problems. They could discuss the difference between an asteroid and a comet.

- Put yourself in the mixing and milling as well. Position yourself so that when you ask the question, you're in close proximity to a student or students who are either struggling with content or ready for a higher-level discussion. If you make sure you get to talk with that student or students, you'll have a perfect opportunity for some small-group reteaching or, perhaps, a more in-depth discussion of content.

- After a few minutes, start the music again. Once again have students mill about the room and then freeze when you stop the music. Repeat the rest of the process, having students form different-sized groups by varying the questions you ask. If you ask "What is 2 x 2?" then students would form groups of four.

NOW LOOK WHAT YOU'VE DONE!

You've got students moving and reviewing content, and you've given yourself a chance to do a real quick assessment. As long as you do something with what you learned from your assessment, that's differentiation!

Now It's Your Turn to Reflect on This Chapter

Are you encouraged that you can begin your journey into differentiating in a whole-group setting with some of these strategies? Keep in mind the fact that in a whole-group setting, we need to do more than just talk to students if we want them to attain personal mastery of concepts, gain real understanding, and develop skills. As you begin to differentiate instruction in your whole-group setting, a good first step is to think about how you can engage all of your students while also creating different pathways for those who need that additional support.

I'd like to suggest you stop now and take the time for some reflection and action planning. Why am I asking you to make some specific plans? Well, chances are you're not reading this book while sitting at your desk with your students in your room. If you *are* sitting and reading this book with a bunch of students in your room, you're probably considering early retirement. I'd imagine that you're home or somewhere else.

Wherever you are, if you don't spend a few minutes in reflection and action planning, chances are you'll put the book down and go to your other life (pick up a child, cook dinner, go to a meeting, etc.) or you'll start doing schoolwork (grading papers, making lesson plans, etc.). Then when you decide to pick up this book again, you will have forgotten what you read.

On the other hand, if you spend a few minutes reflecting and planning after you read each chapter, then you can quickly look and see what impacted you the most as you read. You're creating your plan. (I'm differentiating a little for you and *your* needs now!) So, pick up a pen or pencil and fill in the blanks.

What is your "aha!" or insight or thinking after reading this chapter?

_____

_____

_____

_____

What strategy will you try first?

How and why might you tailor one of the strategies in this chapter to meet the needs of a specific student or students?

Questioning Window

You may be wondering why in the world this book would include a chapter on questioning. It's not news that questioning is an important part of teaching. But think about this a minute. In your upper-grade classroom, you're at the mercy of a bell that rings every 45, 55, 75, or 90 minutes. As soon as the bell rings, that class leaves and another one appears. You want to do a good job, and you want all of your students to be successful —but you have to manage that in those 45-, 55-, 75-, or 90-minute blocks.

So you fall into the habit of viewing yourself as the one who must move the instruction forward. If the students ask questions, that's an interruption; there just isn't enough time in a class period for a lot of questions. As a result, you become the main question asker.

Then you begin to think that the main goal of asking questions at all is to assess the performance of the students. If that's the case, you decide (consciously or not) that maybe questions are best left to a quiz at the end of a unit or the end of a class period. You go on to assume that during class in the whole-group setting, there is time only to ask students if everyone understands or if there are any questions. Heaven forbid that somebody *does* have a question—that would interrupt the learning process!

But what if that *is* the learning process?

Have you ever asked your class, "Are there any questions?" and had students just sit there and stare at you in total silence? Have you ever asked, "Does everyone understand?" and had students bob their heads up and down? You probably think everything about your instruction is very clear to your students. But do you know what the head bobbing really means?

It means that their neck muscles are moving.

That's all it means. What those students are really thinking, if they are engaged at all, is that if you continue teaching, then they will begin to understand at some point.

In a setting like this, students become reluctant to interrupt you and ask questions. In a whole-group setting, it's easy to de-emphasize questioning and to let it become a secondary vehicle of your instruction. The primary vehicle is you, the sage on the stage, constantly reconstructing a text or problem for your students. You, not the students, are creating an understanding of the content that goes beyond just the surface.

STUDENT-CENTERED INSTRUCTION

But remember: differentiation is student centered and not teacher centered. Exactly what does "student centered" mean? It means the focus is off you and on your students. It means students are *doing* something, as opposed to just sitting and listening.

Please don't misunderstand me. I'm not suggesting you're doing things wrong. But I *am* suggesting that instruction in your whole-group setting will be even more effective if you give some more thought to the questioning that takes place—both the questions you ask and the questions the students generate.

Good questioning engages students, helps them construct meaning, and develops higher-level thinking skills. How can your students remember and use what they're learning if the only time they open their mouths is to yawn? (Of course, yawning is exactly what you'll get if your primary vehicle for instruction is teacher talk!)

That brings me to another consideration. Which do you think is more important in your classroom: the question or the answer?

You might say, "Well, I present the curriculum to my whole class in the best way I know how, and the majority of them can answer the questions I ask. I've taught it, and I assume that if they answer my questions, then they've learned it. So the answer is more important."

But what if I said to you that there is more thinking and learning going on when students are asking questions?

Consider entrepreneur and inventor

George Ballas of Houston, Texas. For years Mr. Ballas was frustrated because he couldn't get rid of the weeds that grew around the trunks of the trees in his yard. Mr. Ballas went through school and played the question-and-answer game, just as I did and just as you probably did. He learned how to give the answers the teacher wanted. However, Mr. Ballas was a little different from the rest of us.

He also asked the question.

When he was having his car washed one day, Mr. Ballas noticed how the car-wash brushes washed all around the outside of his car, managing to clean the car without damaging it. So he asked himself: "Is there something I could make that would operate on this same concept—something that would help me get rid of the weeds around the trunks of my trees without damaging the trees?"

George Ballas is the inventor of the Weedeater string trimmer. Millions of Americans have Weedeater trimmers to help keep their yards looking nice—and Mr. Ballas has millions of dollars in the bank! Before I purchased a Weedeater, I was frustrated with the weeds in my yard just as Mr. Ballas had been. But I didn't ask the question.

THE QUESTION IS MORE IMPORTANT THAN THE ANSWER

But you know what research has shown? On average, teachers ask 80 questions each hour. Can you guess how many questions students ask in that same time period?

Two.

Yep: two (Kagan, 1999). And that's two questions for the entire class, so that means most kids aren't asking *any* questions. There are reasons why that happens, and we've talked about them already. But my point is this: Think about what an opportunity you have as a teacher! If you can force yourself to ask for *questions* from your students instead of always calling for answers, think how much more they could learn!

By the way, have you noticed that when the students are the ones coming up with the questions, they're automatically differentiating themselves? For example, when studying capital punishment, a struggling student might ask, "What is capital punishment?" and a more advanced student might ask, "Could we talk about whether capital punishment is right? Here's what I think and I can support my view."

Or course there will still be times when you do need to be the one asking the questions. Those are the times when you need to think about something else: the *kinds* of questions you're asking. Remember when you were in school and you learned about Bloom's Taxonomy? You probably studied the different levels of thinking, and somebody probably drummed it into your head that you need to emphasize the questions from the higher end of the scale.

You remember those higher-level questions, right? The synthesis and evaluation questions that require students to understand and apply information? As opposed to the knowledge and comprehension questions that call for memorized answers?

Those higher-level thinking skills are more important than ever today, for a reason Benjamin Bloom would never have thought of: more and more of them are showing up on accountability assessments. Knowing that, can you guess what kinds of questions teachers are asking their students?

Research has shown that, in classrooms all across America, 80% of the questions teachers ask are at the knowledge and comprehension level (Johnson, 1995).

So here's another opportunity. If you can get yourself to ask higher-level questions and if you can get your students to ask and answer questions at a higher level, think about how much more learning you could get out of your class time.

WHAT DOES THIS HAVE TO DO WITH DIFFERENTIATING INSTRUCTION ANYWAY?

There's a story that a teacher once asked a student to summarize the life of Socrates in four sentences. The student replied: "Socrates lived a long time ago. He was very intelligent. Socrates gave long speeches. His listeners poisoned him."

Maybe there's a lesson here. Often

teachers tend to "talk at" students because that approach is easier and seems more efficient. It's the way many of us were taught, and it's more organized. However, if more learning occurs when more questioning occurs, and if all of your students need to be pushed to think and process at higher levels, maybe there's a better alternative.

As you consider the wide range of learners in your classroom, sometimes it's appropriate to ask the struggling students questions that simplify the content and to ask the more able students those higher-level questions. For example, you might ask one student to list the characteristics of mammals and another student to compare and contrast mammals with reptiles.

If the question is more important than the answer, then students need to learn to generate questions. Good readers are always asking questions while reading. They're engaged and active while reading, not passively waiting for the teacher to ask the questions at the end. The ability to generate questions is the key to higher levels of learning.

Students can pose questions that come from their interests in content, and you can use those questions to help the students set goals for learning. For example, a student might want to know why certain antibiotics are used to treat certain diseases, why some antibiotics are called "broad spectrum," and how common it is for some antibiotics to cause allergic reactions.

This chapter will give you lots of easy-to-implement strategies for both the questions you ask and the ones the students

generate. But before you continue, I have one other suggestion for you. Try asking a colleague to videotape one of your lessons so you can see how effective your questioning is now. Once you've established that baseline, open this window by turning the page and considering the strategies that follow.

Differentiated Wait Time

Y ou had the class in your teacher preparation that told you it was important to give students "wait time" after asking a question. Why is that important? Thinking takes time. That doesn't fit well with the pressure on you today to get in so much instruction in a limited time. The pressure leads to a hurried pace of instruction, and that in turn leads to a harried environment. Before you realize it, you're firing questions at your students one right after the other.

I know that in my classroom, because I like to keep things moving, I probably gave my students only a couple of seconds of wait time. What's worse is that I probably answered most of the questions I asked my students.

I'll just blame it on my husband. Sometimes when he's slow to answer, I'll answer for him. That behavior became a habit that carried over to the students. Does this sound familiar to you—in your home *or* your classroom? Husbands are probably glad they don't have to respond, but our students are different. Although they might be glad they don't *have* to respond, without sufficient wait time, many students are *unable* to respond. As soon as somebody answers the question, everybody stops thinking.

Finding creative ways to add some wait time to your questioning can make a big difference. That's where this strategy comes in.

CHEW ON IT

For every 8 to 10 minutes of sage-on-the-stage instruction, ask your students to "chew" or process the information in some way. For example, ask students to:

- pair off and discuss with their partners what they've learned.

- participate in a whip—a process of your going around the class and getting quick responses to questions. Just be sure to give your students wait time before you start the whip around.

- play a game such as Wheel of Fortune, Jeopardy, or Hollywood Squares.

No matter which of these approaches you use, just be sure to "chunk" the information—giving students manageable amounts of information at one time—and give them a chance to "chew" on it!

STEP BY STEP

- Give students 5 to 10 seconds to respond to a question. Make sure they know that they're expected to use that time to think about their answers.

- Follow a random method for calling on students. Put kids' names on craft sticks and put the craft sticks in a jar, then randomly pull out a stick and ask the child whose name is on that stick to answer the question. Students will learn that they're all responsible for every question.

- Tell students you're not going to call on anyone until more than half of them have raised their hands.

- Occasionally call on students who don't have their hands raised.

- Ask students to explain how they arrived at their responses, whether or not the response is correct. It's the thinking you're after.

NOW LOOK WHAT YOU'VE DONE!

When you begin to increase wait time in your whole-group setting, you'll notice that the length of student responses increases and failure to respond decreases. When you become less and less the sage on the stage, students ask more questions and begin to interact with one another. You'll find yourself asking questions at a higher level, especially of those students who can handle that, and you'll find that your students make more inferences and start giving more speculative responses. Speculative responses boost creative thinking.

WHO NEEDS DIFFERENTIATED WAIT TIME?

While additional wait time will increase the quality and depth of the answers in general, some wait time may need to be differentiated. Often boys need more wait time than girls. Some students from poverty need more wait time because they have less background knowledge and limited vocabulary. Often English-language learners need additional time to process thoughts in their first language and then to translate into English. Many students with identified learning disabilities need additional time to process and reflect before giving a response.

But what about those students at the other end of the spectrum—the ones you perceive to be highly able? It may surprise you to know that retrieval rates and intelligence are not linked. Sometimes those highly able students in your room have neural networks that are much denser, and their thoughts and responses are more complex (Kingore, 2004). If you call only on the students whose hands are up in the air first, you and your class will miss the deeper thoughts of some of these students.

The Parking Lot & Geometric Questions

Thinking takes time. In the previous strategy, we looked at the wait time you give your students after you ask a question. The Parking Lot and Geometric Questions give your students wait time for coming up with questions and more wait time before you respond. This can particularly benefit certain students from poverty, some English language learners, some boys, and some students with identified learning disabilities.

STEP BY STEP

• Make copies of one or both of the reproducibles on pages 97–98: The Parking Lot and Geometric Questions.

• Give those copies to your students to keep in their notebooks.

• During a unit of study, have students write on those copies any questions they have about the topic. Or they can write their questions on sticky notes and place the sticky notes on copies of the reproducibles.

• Reserve the last part of your class time to respond to all unresolved student questions.

VARIATION

Instead of making copies of the reproducibles for students to keep in their notebooks, enlarge the reproducibles on a copier, laminate them, and use them as posters for the classroom. Then have students write their questions on Post-it notes and stick them on the posters.

NOW LOOK WHAT YOU'VE DONE!

When you allow students to have their own wait time, you're modeling for them that thinking is valued in the classroom.

I Do Have a Question

Here's a strategy that encourages students to ask questions during a class discussion. It also gives you a good way to make sure you're asking questions that go beyond just the knowledge and comprehension levels of questioning. Those students who are reluctant learners, shy, frequently off task, or especially good at "pushing your buttons" are prime candidates for this approach.

STEP BY STEP

- Use the Key Words & Sample Questions from Bloom's Taxonomy (see reproducibles on pages 99–100) to create questions for a unit of study.

- Write several questions on index cards, making sure to include questions from the higher levels.

- Select several students and meet with them privately. Give each of them an index card with a question on it. Ask each student to memorize the question on her card; explain that she shouldn't tell other students that you've given her a question.

- Tell each of the selected students that when he hears you say, "Does anyone have a question?" that's his cue to raise his hand. Call on those students to ask the questions.

NOW LOOK WHAT YOU'VE DONE!

It's easy to see that when you focus on the needs of certain students, you're differentiating your instruction according to how students feel about themselves, the classroom, and learning. That's why you selected particular students to "plant" your questions with. But you're doing more than that.

As you ask questions that invite higher-level thinking, you engage more students because they're manipulating and relating to the content rather than just repeating the content by rote. These kinds of whole-class discussions also serve as models so that students who aren't yet ready to answer at a higher level can benefit from the discussion.

Give Me Five!

Good readers continually ask questions while reading. Poor readers merely move their eyes across the page. The graphic organizer Give Me Five helps students remember five critical questions to ask while reading. This strategy invites those struggling readers to stay focused, engaged, and thinking as they read.

STEP BY STEP

• Make one copy of the larger Give Me Five graphic organizer (see reproducible on page 101) for each student in the class—but don't distribute them yet.

THE FIVE QUESTIONS

1 What mental pictures do I see?
(Visualization)

2 What does this remind me of?
(Connections)

3 What do I know now, even though I wasn't told the information in the text? (Inference)

4 What might happen next?
(Prediction)

5 What was this mostly about?
(Summarization/Conclusions)

• Write on the board the five questions from that organizer.

• To introduce this strategy, ask each student to refer to his appointment calendar (see pages 8–9) and to meet with a partner from a particular time slot.

• Have students touch each finger of their own hands as they share their answers to the five questions in terms of the book they've just read. For example, one student might touch his thumb and say, "Here's one of the mental pictures that I could see while we were reading. I could just see the barn where the animals lived. It was really dirty and old and smelled really yucky."

• Read a book with your students. As you read, stop periodically and model for students how to use the Give Me Five questions with their own reading. If you were reading "Eleven," from *Woman Hollering Creek and Other Stories,* by Sandra Cisneros, you might model something like what appears on page 35.

• Once you're comfortable that students understand how to respond to the questions, give each student a copy of the Give Me Five organizer. Ask each student to write his answers to the questions in the blank spaces of the organizer. If he needs more room, he can use a separate sheet of paper.

I could see the classroom and Rachel. I think she has brown hair and is very short. The classroom is very cluttered.

When I was in third grade, I got in trouble for something I didn't do.

You shouldn't just think something is true without checking it out.

I think the teacher will apologize to Rachel. Everyone can have a bad day—even teachers.

I think this story is mostly about a conflict between a teacher and a student over a red sweater.

VARIATION

Make one copy of the smaller Give Me Five graphic organizer (see reproducible on page 102) for each student. Cut apart and laminate the organizers, then give them to students as reminders of questions to ask while reading.

NOW LOOK WHAT YOU'VE DONE!

You've differentiated for learning styles. As they use the organizer in this way, the visual learners have something to look at, the auditory learners have something to hear or say, and the kinesthetic learners have something to touch.

Question Stems & Cubing

We know that different children have different learning preferences. The way you structure questions can instantly exclude some of your students, or it can invite all of them into the process. To be sure you're including everyone, try beginning your questions with a variety of question stems and using a strategy known as cubing.

Cubing uses a simple visual of an easily constructed cube to approach a topic from multiple directions. You can use cubes in different colors to differentiate according to learning modalities.

STEP BY STEP

- First you need to know how many of each kind of cube you're going to make for your class. To figure that out, think about how you'd group your students according to learning modalities. Assuming that each group will have no more than four students, you need to know how many groups of visual learners you have, how many groups of auditory learners, and how many groups of kinesthetic learners.
- Turn to the reproducibles on pages 103–05. Each section of each of these cube patterns has a command. You'll need to add specific instructions to the

commands to create appropriate tasks for each group.

- Since you may want to come back and re-use the cube patterns later, I'd suggest that your next step should be to make one copy of each of the three learning-styles cubes on plain white paper. Note that you might want to enlarge these on the copier in order to have more room to write.

FOR EXAMPLE

If students have read a narrative, then you might create a cube for visual learners on which the sides read something like this:

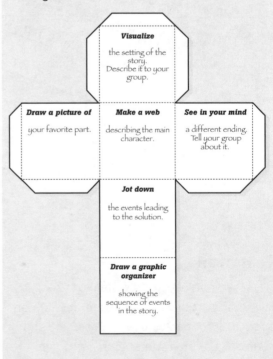

Visualize
the setting of the story. Describe it to your group.

Draw a picture of
your favorite part.

Make a web
describing the main character.

See in your mind
a different ending. Tell your group about it.

Jot down
the events leading to the solution.

Draw a graphic organizer
showing the sequence of events in the story.

- Explain that once each student knows what his task is, he should work on that assignment on his own. However, students can also help each other.

- Finally, ask students to share with one another how they completed their tasks.

VARIATION

Start with the blank cube pattern on page 106 and create new cubes that differentiate by student interests.

NOW LOOK WHAT YOU'VE DONE!

You've used the same strategy for the whole group, but you've varied the details to honor each modality preference. As a result, you've dramatically increased each child's chance to become engaged in learning—and that means you've also increased his chances of succeeding.

- Next, on your copies, add specific task instructions to each section of each cube.

- Go back to the copier with the filled-in cube patterns. Make the appropriate number of cube patterns for each learning modality, using a different color of card stock for each type of cube. Let's say you copy the cube for visual learners onto green card stock, the one for auditory learners onto blue stock, and the one for kinesthetic learners onto yellow stock.

- In class, divide the students into the groups you've decided on. Give each group a cube in the appropriate color. Make sure the students understand what each command means.

- Have the students in each group take turns throwing the cube and noting the instructions listed on the part of the cube that lands face up. Explain that if the student doesn't want to perform that task, he can roll the cube a second time.

Cubing & Bloom's

The previous strategy addressed ways to reach different learning modalities through the cubing strategy. You can also create cubes in which the instructions on each side of the cube correspond to one level of Bloom's Taxonomy. This is a great way to build higher-level thinking skills.

STEP BY STEP

- For a cube pattern, turn to the reproducible on page 107.

- Since you may want to come back and re-use the cube pattern later with other content, make one copy of the pattern on plain white paper. (You might want to use the enlarging feature on the copier in order to give yourself more room to write.)

- See how there are six sides to the pattern, and how each side of the cube pattern has a command? And you know how Bloom's Taxonomy deals with six levels of thinking? I'm so glad Ben made this easy for us! What you're going to do is add specific instructions to each basic command so that you create an appropriate task for each level of thinking.

THE BLOOM'S CUBE

You can make a cube to encourage higher-level thinking by starting with these commands on the six sides of the cube:

Describe . . . (knowledge level)

Explain . . . (comprehension level)

Develop . . . (application level)

Classify . . . (analysis level)

Create a new . . . (synthesis level)

In your opinion . . . (evaluation level)

For example, if students are recycling, the sides of the cube might read:

- Describe the materials being recycled in our school.

- Explain how you surveyed the other students. (This assumes, of course, that the students have *done* a survey.)

- Develop a bar graph showing the results of the survey.

- Classify the different materials being recycled according to categories of your choice.

- Create a new survey on recycling to administer to the community.

- In your opinion, why is more plastic than aluminum being recycled in our school?

- To help students understand the process, try modeling this strategy first with a non-academic topic. For example, make a cube using the commands in the box on page 38 and based on the subject of a clean desk (e.g., "Describe a clean desk," "In your opinion, how important is a clean desk?" etc.). Have students take turns rolling the cube and giving responses. (Alternatively, write the six commands on the board and work with them from there.) You might get some interesting results!

- Once you're sure students understand the process, you can apply the same principle to content. Go back to the copier with the same or another filled-in cube pattern and make enough copies so that you can give one to each student in the class.

- Hand out the copies to students and explain that each student is to respond to each of the six prompts independently (on the cube itself, if she has enough room there, or on a separate sheet of paper if he needs more space). However, anyone can also ask for help from other students or from you if he needs it.

- Ask students to share with one another how they completed their tasks.

Make a web describing the main character.

Jot down the events leading to the solution.

FOR EXAMPLE

Need to see more? Turn to the reproducibles for a math cube and a comprehension cube on pages 108 and 109 respectively.

- Now try out this strategy for yourself! Using the command prompts from the box on page 38, think about your responses to each of the six commands. Your topic is differentiating instruction in a whole-group setting.

VARIATION

Try color coding the Bloom's cubes. Start with the same reproducible, but make extra copies. Fill in the sides of each copy with commands that are appropriate for the various readiness levels, interests, or learning profiles in your class.

NOW LOOK WHAT YOU'VE DONE!

Within the whole group, you've managed to engage all of your students. You've given kinesthetic learners a chance to move around a bit and work with the cube. You've given auditory learners a chance to respond in ways that are meaningful to them, and you've given visual learners a chance to show what they know by reading and writing. At the same time, you've also incorporated higher-level thinking skills in your teaching.

Are you feeling a little bit more at ease about differentiating instruction in a whole-group setting? I hope so. I want you to *open* each window of opportunity—not jump out of it!

I Have/Who Has?

I Have/Who Has? is a great alternative to work sheets for studying and reviewing content. It's quick, gets students engaged immediately, and can be used in any content area.

STEP BY STEP

- Turn to the reproducible on page 110. Make enough copies for each student to get one card.

- Cut the cards apart.

- If you like, laminate the copies so you can re-use them later with different content.

- Fill in the blank spaces so that each card has a question on the bottom and the answer to a different question at the top. Make sure that the question on each card has a corresponding answer on another card.

- Give one card to each student.

- Call on any student to start the game by reading only the question (not the answer) on his card.

- Explain that whoever has the card with the answer to that question should say, "I have [the answer to the question]" and should then ask, "Who has [the question on his card]?" For example, if I'm the first student to start, I might say, "Who has 8 x 8?" The student with the answer

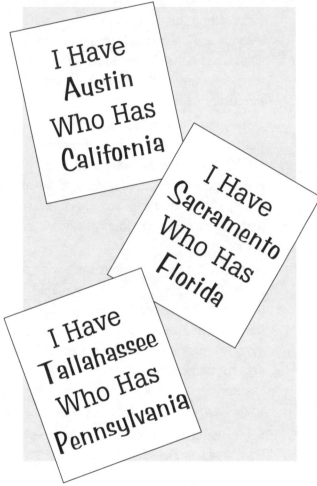

would say, "I have 64. Who has 7 x 3 [or whatever question is on the card]?"

- Continue until the student who started the game is able to give the answer from his card.

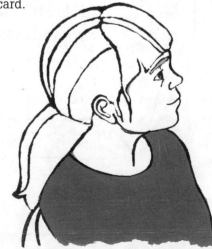

VARIATIONS

Variation 1: I think sometimes it's good to be a little devious. Just think what might happen if you were to "arrange" things so that a particular student received a certain card that would allow him to experience some success. You would be differentiating for the way that student feels about learning and the classroom.

Variation 2: Think of all the possibilities for content you can cover with this strategy. You can work with states and capitals, math facts, equivalent fractions, vocabulary terms and definitions, learning class names, and much more.

NOW LOOK WHAT YOU'VE DONE!

Talk about auditory reinforcement—this strategy has it! It's a great approach for those auditory learners. It also invites all students to be better listeners.

SPEAKING OF LISTENING

Wouldn't you agree that we all could be better listeners? There's a reason each letter in the word "silent" is also in the word "listen." (You're checking me on that right now, aren't you? I can just see you!)

But the Answer's Not Here!

How often do your students say to you, "But the answer is not here!"? Help is on the way! The Question-Answer-Relationship (Q.A.R.) strategy improves the questioning skills of teachers and the comprehension and questioning skills of students. Question-Answer Relationship (Raphael, 1982) is a strategy that considers questions not in isolation but in relation to a piece of text and to a student's knowledge base.

The Q.A.R. strategy lets your students know that they must think in more than one way in order to answer questions from a text. When you ask questions in each of the Q.A.R. categories, you expose students to higher levels of thinking. Better yet, when students are the ones making up questions in each of those categories, *they* are generating questions that call for higher levels of thinking.

STEP BY STEP

- There are two major types of Question-Answer Relationships: In-the-Book questions and In-My-Head questions.

- There are two types of In-the-Book questions:

  ✓ With Right-There questions, the answer is found in one place in the text. In *Goldilocks and the Three Bears*, a Right-There question would be, "What did Mama Bear pour in the bowls?"

  ✓ Think, Search, and Find questions go one step further. With these, the answer is found in different places in the text. A Think, Search, and Find question would be, "Where did Goldilocks go inside the bears' house?"

- There are also two types of In-My-Head questions:

  ✓ For Author-and-Me questions, the answer is not found in the text, but the text still has to be read. While reading, the student must look for clues and evidence in the text and then combine those with the student's own background knowledge to figure out the answer. "How did Goldilocks feel when she saw the three bears?" would be an Author-and-Me question.

  ✓ An On-My-Own question is not dependent on the text. Rather the answer comes from the student's prior knowledge. For example: "Have you ever known that someone else has been in your bedroom at home? How did you know?" You have a reason for teaching this last category, even though it relies on prior knowledge and not on the text. If you don't teach students the different types of questions, then they sometimes tend to answer everything as if it were an On-My-Own question. Teach this category so that you can point out these things to students later.

- Copy the reproducibles from pages 111–15, using the enlarging feature on the copier to make the copies as big as possible. Laminate the posters and then hang them in your classroom.

- Teach the Q.A.R. strategy with a variety of reading selections. Children's picture books are great for introducing older students to this approach because with these books the students don't get bogged down in the content while learning the strategy.

- Once you're sure students understand the four types of questions, have them begin to generate their own questions in the Q.A.R. format.

- Hold all students accountable for making up each of the types of questions, but tier or level the activity according to their readiness or reading levels. Those students below grade level might use children's picture books to make up their questions, the on-grade-level students could use on-grade-level texts to make up their questions, and the above-grade-level students could use graphs or charts or some type of non-standard text to generate their questions.

NOW LOOK WHAT YOU'VE DONE!

Once students are familiar with this strategy, when a student comes to you and says, "But the answer's not here!" you can reply, "Maybe that's not a Right-There question!"

FOR EXAMPLE

Sample text like this, which will engage the sports fans in your class, provides a great way to introduce the Q.A.R. strategy.

Baseball players and their fans are always interested in batting averages. Batting averages are used to measure the hitting performance of the players. To figure a batting average, you divide the number of hits a player has by the batter's official at bats. An official at bat does not include the number of times the batter has hit a sacrifice fly, walked, or been hit by a pitch. So if a player has 10 hits and 50 official at bats, the batting average would be calculated as follows: 10 divided by 50 is equal to .200. Batting averages are always recorded as three-digit decimals.

Another reason batting averages are important is that they are used to help determine the hitting order of the team. A batting average of .300 or above is considered very good in major league baseball.

Batting averages are frequently reported in chart form, like this:

This Season	At Bats	Singles	Doubles	Triples	Home Runs	Average
Player A	400	65	25	3	4	.243
Player B	397	70	30	2	9	.279
Player C	395	75	36	6	11	.324

Once students have read the text and chart, pose these questions:

Right There: How is a batting average calculated? (The answer is in one place in the text.)

Think, Search, and Find: How are batting averages used? (The answer is in several places in the text.)

Author and Me: How much higher is Player C's batting average than Player A's? (This question is text dependent. The student must read the text/chart, looking for clues and evidence in the form of the numbers on the chart. He then must combine that information with what is "in his head"—the process of subtraction—to figure out the answer.)

On My Own: Are you a baseball fan? (The answer to this question is not dependent upon the text.)

Strategy #9

Question-Tac-Toe

A Question-Tac-Toe is a menu of
questions that can help students
think at different levels of Bloom's
taxonomy. This strategy also allows you to
differentiate assignments over the course of a
unit of study. By using a menu like this, you
give students a chance to participate in activities or create end products appropriate for
their individual learning styles.

STEP BY STEP

• On the Question-Tac-Toe grid (see
  reproducibles on pages 116–19),
  create a menu of possible activities, questions, and/or end products students can respond to. Post
  the grid on a bulletin board in
  your classroom or use it as a
  handout for each student.

• Have the students choose at least
  three of the questions—perhaps
  one from each line—to answer
  over a period of time.

VARIATION

In order to differentiate the
Question-Tac-Toes based on your students' readiness, their interests, or
how they learn, assign students different questions to answer.

NOW LOOK WHAT YOU'VE DONE!

A Question-Tac-Toe can be a wonderful
way to honor individual learning styles and
readiness levels.

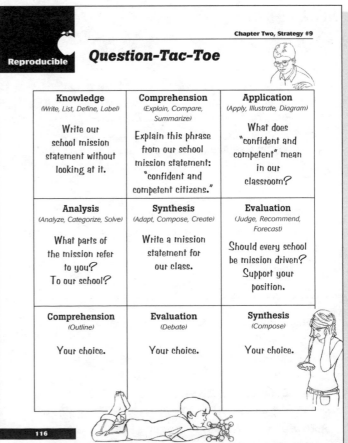

Chapter Two, Strategy #9

Reproducible

Question-Tac-Toe

Knowledge (Write, List, Define, Label)	Comprehension (Explain, Compare, Summarize)	Application (Apply, Illustrate, Diagram)
Write our school mission statement without looking at it.	Explain this phrase from our school mission statement: "confident and competent citizens."	What does "confident and competent" mean in our classroom?
Analysis (Analyze, Categorize, Solve)	**Synthesis** (Adapt, Compose, Create)	**Evaluation** (Judge, Recommend, Forecast)
What parts of the mission refer to you? To our school?	Write a mission statement for our class.	Should every school be mission driven? Support your position.
Comprehension (Outline)	**Evaluation** (Debate)	**Synthesis** (Compose)
Your choice.	Your choice.	Your choice.

116

D.E.A.Q.

Key words and sample questions can encourage both you and your students to generate questions that address a wide range of thinking skills. D.E.A.Q. stands for Drop Everything And Question.

STEP BY STEP

- Turn to the reproducibles for Key Words & Sample Questions from Bloom's Taxonomy (pages 99-100) and make one copy of those pages for each student in the class.

- Hand out those copies to the students, and assign different levels of questions to individuals or groups of students. Explain that their task is to come up with a written set of questions that are at the assigned level and relate to a specific topic of study.

- Set a timer for 5–10 minutes and challenge students to see how many questions everyone can generate in the time given.

- That includes you! Do the same thing the students are doing at the same time they're doing it. I'd suggest that you assign yourself one of the higher levels.

- Collect all the questions. Look through what you've collected and choose appropriate questions to include in class discussions, on assessments, as journal topics, or for group discussions. Of course, include some of your own questions in the mix.

NOW LOOK WHAT YOU'VE DONE!

You've differentiated the level of questions you assigned certain students according to their readiness for the content. By directing the more in-depth and challenging question assignments to the students who are ready for that kind of complexity, and asking other students to generate those questions that simplify the content, you're helping everyone to succeed. You can apply this same kind of differentiation (readiness for content) when you ask individual students or groups of students to respond to questions the class has generated.

FOR EXAMPLE

Math: Imagine there were no more circles. Write two paragraphs about what life would be like. (synthesis)

Science: List all the ways you can think of in which matter and energy interact. (knowledge)

Social studies: Explain the effect of the assassination of President John Kennedy on the people of the United States. (comprehension)

Literacy: Compare and contrast the story with another one you have read. (analysis)

T.H.I.N.K.

I f you want a fun and exciting questioning tool, include T.H.I.N.K. questions in your daily teaching. T.H.I.N.K. stands for Thoughts, How Come, What If, Name and Next, Kind of Alike and Kind of Different. Remember that in a differentiated classroom, you want to challenge *all* students to think creatively and at higher levels. Involving all students in answering these questions will help you do that. What may differ is how you get each student to the higher levels.

FOR EXAMPLE

T is for Thoughts/Feelings/Opinion/Point of View Questions: "In your opinion, should junk food be banned from vending machines?"

H is for How Come Questions: "How come a slim chance and a fat chance are the same thing?"

I is for What If Questions: "What if your mom had your dad's job and your dad had your mom's job?"

N is for both Name and Next Questions: "Name all the ways you can make ten." "Lightning has just knocked out all the electricity in your home. What do you do next?"

K is for Kind of Alike and Kind of Different Questions: "How are a cat and a bird different?" "How are a guitar and a puppy alike?"

STEP BY STEP

• Pose a question from each of the T.H.I.N.K. categories once a day. The box on this page has some examples to get you started; you'll find more in the reproducibles on pages 120–22.

• Use these questions for warm-up activities, for transition times (e.g., waiting in line), and as anchor activities (assignments that the rest of the class works on when you need to give your attention to a smaller group of students).

• You can further differentiate this strategy by having some of the more academically able students make up their own T.H.I.N.K. questions. Or you can challenge those students by combining some of the T.H.I.N.K. questions. For example, you might say, "Name all the items you can think of that might have been on a wagon if the westward movement had taken place in 2004." (That would be a combination of a Name Question with a What If Question.)

NOW LOOK WHAT YOU'VE DONE!

T.H.I.N.K. questions will bring out positive emotions in all of your students. And you'll be surprised at the insightful responses and the higher-level thinking you'll get.

Talk with F.R.E.D.

Have you ever noticed that it's often hard to question your students in a whole-group setting in a way that will really guide them through the steps of critical thinking? What you need is a cheat sheet. That's where "Talk with F.R.E.D." comes in.

STEP BY STEP

- Before students read a text or watch a presentation or video, write a list of questions that you want to ask the class, based on the Talk with F.R.E.D. guidelines. (See the reproducible on page 123 for sample questions for each step.) Concentrate on open-ended questions. Be sure to tailor the questions to the subject and to the group of students.

- After the class reads the text or is otherwise introduced to new content, ask your questions. Following the Talk with F.R.E.D. format will help you stimulate a meaningful discussion.

- Spend three to four minutes at each step of questioning.

- Ask students to elaborate on their answers by giving specific examples.

- This strategy is also useful with small groups and with individual students. For example, try meeting one-on-one with a struggling student and using this strategy to get him to broaden his perspectives,

INTRODUCING F.R.E.D.

Facts: These are questions that get at what students have seen, heard, or experienced.

Reflections: These are questions that get your students' emotions involved by finding out how they feel.

Evaluation: These questions invite your students to make meaning.

Decisions: These questions help with decisions.

gain insight, and make a better plan. In that case, you might ask:

- ✓ **Facts**: What are your grades? What is your study routine? Why do you suppose you're struggling?

- ✓ **Reflections**: How do you feel about your grades?

- ✓ **Evaluation**: What does it mean if you fail a subject? What impact could failing have on your goals?

- ✓ **Decisions**: What plan can you make to reverse this situation?

NOW LOOK WHAT YOU'VE DONE!

One of the traits you can differentiate for is how your students feel about the learning experience. Use this strategy to communicate to students that you care, but also to show that in the classroom, the responsibility for learning is shared. Shared responsibility means that students set learning goals and become active, contributing members of the class.

Planning Questions Are the Key

The key to successful differentiation is knowing your individual students. You need to know each student's readiness, how he learns best, what interests him, and what he thinks and feels about the classroom. If you know those things, you can help students succeed in your whole-group setting by proactively planning when, how, and for which students you need to differentiate.

Does this mean you do this all the time, 24 hours a day, with every unit and with every student? No. But it does mean that you are conscious of what will work and what won't work for each student.

STEP BY STEP

- We've talked about how you can differentiate when you question your students. Now let's take a look at questions you can ask *yourself* as you plan your instruction that will help you to differentiate in your classroom.

- Consider the content or the "what" of your teaching and how your students access that content. Ask yourself these questions:

  ✓ What are the standards I'm addressing and assessing in this content?

  ✓ What are the concepts and skills to be mastered?

  ✓ Is there a guiding question or questions that might shape the study of this content?

  ✓ How can I make this content relevant to my students?

  ✓ How will I figure out what the students already know? What will I do with that data? How can I help them build on prior experiences?

  ✓ What would be appropriate and meaningful ways for students to gain access to this content? How can I engage the students and not just lecture the majority of the time? (Possibilities might include Internet research, field trips, simulations, and guest speakers.)

- Think about the process or the activities the students engage in to make meaning of the content. Ask yourself:

  ✓ When students are involved in an activity, is it leading to their mastery of the content?

  ✓ Are the activities in which students are involved related to the guiding questions and the curricula goals of this unit of study? (This is important. If you don't think about this, you might find you are planning activities that aren't related to the goals of the unit of study.)

  ✓ Do the activities I've planned for this unit of study challenge the students appropriately and require them to think critically about the content?

- ✓ Are the activities engaging and meaningful to students?

- ✓ Am I using multiple resources to teach this content?

- ✓ Do the materials and activities I'm using address a wide range of reading levels and learning profiles, and do they reflect the particular interests of my students this year?

- ✓ Am I building in some choices for students in terms of how they work and what activities they engage in?

• Move on to the product or the ways your students show you what they've learned. Ask yourself these questions:

- ✓ How will my students show that they've mastered the content?

- ✓ Will the ways my students show that they've mastered the content involve higher levels of thinking as well as in-depth understanding?

- ✓ Will the products my students develop encourage them to integrate and apply what they've learned?

- ✓ Could I work with all my students to establish class criteria for success with products?

- ✓ Could I work with individual students to help each add his own personal criteria?

- ✓ Could my students have some choice as to how they'll express their learning?

• Take a look at the learning environment of your classroom. Ask yourself these questions:

- ✓ Have I talked with my students about the fact that we all learn differently?

- ✓ Are my students aware of classroom agreements, responsibilities, and procedures so that our learning together will proceed smoothly?

- ✓ As I reflect on my plans, am I appropriately challenging each of my students, making sure that they can all be successful in a safe and caring learning environment?

FOR EXAMPLE

If you're teaching fourth-grade science, and you know that some of your students (those visual/spatial types) really love to draw, ask those students to draw the water cycle and label the parts. Ask the students who seem more "active" (those bodily/kinesthetic types) to act out the water cycle, and those students who excel in language arts (those verbal/linguistic types) to write a report on the water cycle.

NOW LOOK WHAT YOU'VE DONE!

In a differentiated classroom, you're committed to meeting the needs of all your students. This is a very different mind set from just operating from the teacher's edition and hoping most of the students "get it." Start small—you can do it!

Now It's Your Turn to Reflect on This Chapter

What is your "aha!" or insight or thinking after reading this chapter?

_____

_____

_____

_____

_____

_____

_____

What strategy will you try first?

_____

_____

_____

_____

_____

How and why might you tailor one of the strategies in this chapter to meet the needs of a specific student or students?

_____

_____

_____

_____

_____

_____

_____

_____

_____

_____

_____

_____

_____

_____

_____

_____

_____

_____

3 Chapter 3

Flexible Grouping Window

I bet you're thinking that this title really sounds crazy! How can you possibly have grouping if you have a whole group?

It all changes when you add the word "flexible."

When I went to school, the standard approach was that everyone sat in rows in classrooms most of the day. We had little or no "legal" interaction with our classmates (we had plenty of "illegal" interaction whenever the teacher wasn't watching) and very little variety of groupings. We listened to lectures with the same (whole) group of students for the majority of each school day. I would label this type of grouping as fixed and not flexible.

Now fast forward to today's classrooms. In many cases, you'll find that same familiar pattern. If you're a teacher in one of those classrooms, I'm sure your heart is in the right place; you want all of your students to be successful. But you might have a relatively small block of time and a room of twenty-plus students with varied backgrounds and skills. Some might be ready for an in-depth study of the theme of a novel, some might struggle to make it through the novel, and a few won't even read it. (The students in that last group are the ones who have learned to fake read and fake listen most of the time.)

You think teaching to their individual needs sounds great. But that clock on the classroom wall is ticking, and you have a lot of content to cover. Whole-class instruction usually requires less preparation time than a less traditional approach. So to get everything in, you usually resort to the familiar method of whole-class instruction for the block of time you have.

This chapter will show you that you do have another option: flexible grouping. Flexible grouping is the practice of grouping students according to their learning needs and the goals of a particular lesson. This is not the same kind of grouping we had when I went to school; in those days, we had groups, but they were set in stone. Once you were in a group, for the most part that was the group you stayed in.

Flexible groups are set in Jell-O.

They're for the short term. Once each individual learner's needs and learning goals are met, the groups dissolve—just like the Jell-O. Just as you don't make Jell-O every day, you don't necessarily use flexible grouping every day. Groups are formed and re-formed as appropriate for particular activities.

For example, one day you might start out in the whole group to watch a video, then break up into smaller, differentiated groups for the follow-up, and finally return to the whole group to share the products from the smaller groups. The fluid and flexible groups that are created could last five minutes or they could last a whole class period. It all depends on the needs of the learners and the objectives of the lesson.

You're probably freaking out right now, thinking, "Wait a minute! I bought this book thinking it was going to show me how to differentiate instruction totally in a whole-group setting!" Don't freak out. You're not giving up on teaching students in a whole-group situation. You're going to vary the grouping patterns at certain times—not every day. Think of it as having subdivisions within your whole group. Rest assured: you can do this!

TYPES OF GROUPS

What are some of the groupings that could occur in your whole group setting? Let's take a look at a few possibilities:

- **Whole group**: Clearly, this is one way to group students. The whole-group approach can often be the most effective choice when you're introducing new concepts, leading a discussion, facilitating a class debate, demonstrating how to do something, giving directions, or getting students involved in a class or team-building activity.

- **Small groups of varying degrees of readiness (heterogeneous)**: This type of grouping works well when students are involved in cooperative learning activities, when they need to learn from one another, or when the goal is building social and collaborative skills.

- **Small groups of like readiness (homogeneous)**: This type of grouping works well when the goal is for students who have similar levels of readiness in a skill or subject to work together.

- **Independent or individual work**: You are used to this grouping arrangement. When your students are being assessed for mastery of content, or when they're practicing a skill, this is the grouping you probably use. Individualizing can also be used for contracts, projects, centers, etc.

GENERAL GROUPING GUIDELINES

That's the theory—but you want to know how to actually do this in your classroom. Let's talk about practicalities. And let's start with some general grouping guidelines.

I'd suggest that you begin by assessing your current grouping practices. If you're departmentalized and work with a team of teachers, think about a class in a specific period—say, your second period class. If you teach the same group of students all day, then think about your class as a whole. Consider a week's time and reflect on what percentage of the time is devoted to whole-group instruction, what percentage to small-group instruction, and what percentage to individual students working independently. The percentages must add up to 100%.

I would imagine that if you bought this book, you'll say that the majority of your classroom time will be devoted to whole-group instruction. As you get more and more comfortable with differentiating instruction and as your students get more and more diverse, the percentage of time devoted to small-group instruction should begin to increase.

One way to think about flexible grouping in your whole-group setting might be to think about having your whole class together at the

 beginning of a lesson. This is good for initiating activities and building a sense of community. During a lesson, students might work in a variety of groupings as they make sense of the content at different rates and at varied levels of complexity.

Maybe you want your class to read the same text, but your students require varying levels of support. In that case, you might take those students for whom the reading won't be difficult, and have them read either independently or with a small group. You might need to read with those students for whom it will be difficult to read the text independently. Still others—those who are primarily auditory learners—might prefer to listen to a recorded version of the text if that's available. At the conclusion of a lesson, you'd have your class come together again to discuss what they've learned and identify further questions or topics for future study.

How do you make the groups in your classroom more flexible and fluid? In the beginning, it may take a conscious effort on your part to avoid always grouping by your students' readiness for certain content. But you can do it.

Consider grouping by what students are interested in or how they learn. For example, during a unit on fractions, students might start out in readiness groups according to what they already know about fractions. Then, at a later point in this unit, you might give students a choice of working on fractions involv-

---

GROUP NAMES MATTER

I've found that it helps, when grouping students by their readiness for content, to name the groups in a way that reflects the content being taught: the "Punctuation Club," the "Double Digit Addition Club," the "Keyboarding Clinic," or the "Times Table Club." Refer to students as groups, clubs, work teams, clinics, pairs, triads, or quads.

When I was in school—and you may be able to relate to this—the common practice was to have three set groups. Often those groups were called something like the "Robins," "Bluebirds," or "Buzzards." The groupings never changed; once you were a Buzzard, you stayed a Buzzard. And if you're a Buzzard forever, what's going on is really tracking; students stay in the same groups day after day and, in some cases, year after year.

ing cooking, carpentry, or money. Grouping by students' interests would then change the student groupings so that individuals are never identified with a single skill or readiness group throughout an entire unit of study.

GROUP SIZE

You'll also need to make some decisions about group size. Some of the options you might want to use at different times are:

- **Pairs**: Pairing can maximize participation and achievement if sharing between the two students is timed (see the strategy Timed-Pair Paraphrase, on page 10).

- **Triads or quads**: These add more ideas to be considered. They also give you options for creating groups that are more diverse in terms of learning profiles, interests, and social skills. For example, you could have three students with different learning profiles work together to create an "expanded" definition of a vocabulary term or concept. Let's say the term is *photosynthesis*. The visual/spatial student might draw the process, the bodily/kinesthetic student might act it out, and the musical student might create a rap about it.

- **Groups of five**: Have you ever heard the expression, "In groups of five, students can hide"? To prevent this, if you use groups of five or more, it's important to structure participation. (See the strategy Numbered Heads Together, on page 63, as an example of structured group participation.)

BUILDING IN ACCOUNTABILITY FOR GROUP WORK

Group work in your classroom will be successful only if you set it up to include both group and individual accountability. Group accountability means that the success of the group depends on the success

of all members of the group. Students must have an underlying commitment to the effort and success of the group. Individual accountability means that the success of the individual members is independent of the success or failure of others.

Here are some of the ways you can incorporate both individual and group accountability in your classroom:

- Have each group complete an evaluation of how well the group functioned. (See the reproducibles for How Well Did We Work Together? and Participation Pizza on pages 124–25.)

- Have each group develop working agreements or norms (see the reproducible for Group Norms on page 126) as well as a list of roles and responsibilities of each group member.

- Discuss with students issues such as what to do or say to a group member who is not choosing to do her part, or ways to become more tolerant of the student who wants to overachieve. Class time is well spent when you and your class decide on comments that encourage one another.

FOR EXAMPLE

In the case of a group member who is choosing not to do his part, a member might say, "It takes all of us working together to achieve our goal. Can I help you to keep us all on the right track?" Or in the case of the group member who wants to overachieve, someone might make a statement such as "You're really helping us achieve our group goal. Each of us needs to have a part in this. Could you watch and help each member as we work toward our goal?"

What's important is for students to understand what it means to encourage one another. It helps to brainstorm and role play ways to convey that encouragement.

A MANAGEMENT TIP

Establish a variety of fun and novel ways to select group leaders. You can always have students count off and then use a spinner to select a group leader by number. However, you might also want to consider the following alternative ways to identify the leader:

- student with the shortest first name or last name
- tallest student, shortest student, etc.
- student wearing the most red, blue, etc.
- student with the most brothers, sisters, siblings
- student with the fewest siblings
- student who most recently ate pizza
- student with the closest birthday
- student who lives farthest from the school
- student who is most colorfully dressed

You also need to plan for individual accountability. Here are some ways to do *that*:

- Have each group member complete an individual task that you can assess.
- Weight the final grades so that the individual assessments are worth more than the group work. For example, you might decide that individual work is worth 80% of a grade and group work is worth 20%. In this way, you won't be punishing those students who do their personal best.

YOUR ROLE: COACH AND FACILITATOR

As you begin your journey into more flexible approaches to grouping, think of yourself as both a coach and a facilitator of learning in your classroom. At times some students might need to attend a "coaching clinic" with you for some instructional support. Maybe your class is working on developing ideas in their writing. You notice that a few students seem to need some additional strategies for elaborating on their ideas. You invite those students to a "coaching clinic," in which you provide them with additional strategies.

At other times your role might be to act as the facilitator of the various groups working in your room. As a facilitator of learning, your job at *those* times is to support all students in doing their best work and their best thinking. You might tell students the focus of a unit of study and then ask them their particular areas of interest within that broad focus. Students could then work with like-interest groups to explore the content.

Another time, you might offer students a menu of choices for approaching a particular

assignment and then conference with them to help them with their choices. This behavior is very different from the continual sage-on-the-stage approach to instruction.

WHAT DOES THIS HAVE TO DO WITH DIFFERENTIATING INSTRUCTION ANYWAY?

An old story has it that a father once told his son that he was very proud of the child for being at the top of his class. The son replied, "It really doesn't matter. They teach us the same thing at both ends!"

Flexible grouping is at the heart of differentiating instruction. It's difficult, if not impossible, to really meet the needs of each of your students without using a variety of grouping patterns in your classroom. Varying the grouping allows you to teach to your students' strengths by considering intelligences, skills, readiness, and interests as you establish each group. To put it another way: Do you want to increase student achievement? Vary the grouping structures within whatever time block you have.

Variety is the key. Any decisions that you make about using flexible groups will of course be driven by student needs and the objectives of the lesson. However, any grouping strategy can be overused. When you vary the grouping patterns you're not only giving yourself a chance to observe your students in a variety of contexts, but you're also helping your students to see themselves and each other in ways that expand—rather than limit—their views of the content and of one another.

One issue that always surfaces when you begin using flexible groupings in your whole-class setting is "What do the rest of the students do if I need to meet with a small group of students?" In the language of differentiation, the term that is used to answer that question is anchoring.

"Anchor activities" are things that students can work on during a class period, unit of study, grading period, or longer. Anchor activities need to be related to content, meaningful, and challenging to students—and they need to be things for which students are held accountable. Anchor activities are *not* the same as what we used to call "seat work," which often was just busywork.

In this chapter, you'll find practical strategies that lend themselves to the variety of grouping options discussed above. And since flexible grouping often means planning meaningful strategies for students who are not part of a group at a particular time, I'm including suggestions for anchor activities as well.

SAMPLE GROUP ROLES

This is a basic list. You and your class may want to add other possibilities.

- **Leader**: Keeps group going; facilitates group work
- **Timekeeper**: Monitors the time
- **Materials manager**: Gets all necessary materials for the group
- **Recorder**: Pulls together or summarizes in writing the work of the group
- **Reporter**: Summarizes the work of the group orally for the rest of the class
- **Scout**: Seeks information from other groups
- **Encourager**: Encourages each member to do his best work

Fair & Equal Are Not the Same

In a differentiated classroom it's important for students to understand that fairness means everyone will get what he needs to be successful. Different groups will often be working on different tasks, so students, as well as parents, need to realize that you have high expectations for everyone in the classroom. They need to know you're not changing the standards everyone must meet, but you're being very deliberate about making the curriculum accessible to each student.

TAKE YOUR CHOICE

You have several options for getting this point across from the beginning. Only you know which of these approaches is likely to work best in your classroom.

- **Metaphor**: Use a metaphor to explain that fair does not necessarily mean equal. Dress up like a doctor, complete with a toy stethoscope and white coat. Tell students that your name is Dr. Quackmeyer and that you're going to cure all their illnesses. Let individual students make up illnesses. One might say he has a headache, another a stomachache, backache, or toothache. Tell students to be in your office at 2 PM and explain that then you'll give a shot to each student. Lead them to understand that you're treating everyone equally, but not fairly. Not every student would necessarily need a shot for his illness. Discuss with them the fact that at times they might not all be doing the same work in the same way, but that they'll all be doing what's needed for each to be successful.

- **T-chart**: Construct a T-chart of what fair looks like and what fair sounds like.

assume responsibility for a different part of the project. Some students in each group might choose to write reports while others might want to be in charge of presenting the reports to the class.

- **Literature**: Find stories or passages in literature that describe examples of fairness. One I especially like is Judy Blume's *The Pain and the Great One*, which is a story about two siblings told from the point of view of each one.

NOW LOOK WHAT YOU'VE DONE!

By using any of these strategies with your students before you start differentiating, you make sure that students (and parents!) understand the basic concept of differentiated instruction. Better yet, by participating in any of these activities, students have already had a little taste of what it's all about.

- **Journal prompts**: Ask students to reflect on and write in their journals about experiences with friends and siblings around the issue of fairness.

- **Concept map**: Work with students to develop a concept map of fairness. (See Concept Map reproducible on page 127.)

- **Project designs**: Challenge groups of students to design projects in which each member of the group participates in a way that's fair to all. Maybe each member could use her particular strengths to

Brainstorming A-Z

This is a very simple strategy that can be used in a variety of ways in a whole-group setting. Try this approach to get students to link what they think they know to what they are about to learn, to invite active listening, and to review content.

TAKE YOUR CHOICE

Give each individual or pair of students a copy of the reproducible Brainstorming A-Z (see page 128). Then try any of these alternatives:

• Make a list: Ask each individual or group to write down, for each letter of the alphabet, a word that's related to the topic of study. For example, when beginning a unit on geometry, students might write angle for A and circle for C, etc.

• Invite active listening: Before reading a selection aloud to the entire class, talk with the students about the topic, then ask them to generate a list. The list should include all the words they can think of that might appear in the text to be read and that begin with a specific letter on the Brainstorming A-Z sheet. For example, if you are reading an article on the problems of childhood obesity, ask your students to brainstorm all the words that start with a "c" and might be included in the article. Students might list words such as calorie, candy, and carbohydrates.

• Review content: After studying a topic, have students work in pairs. Ask each person to use the reproducible as a framework to list all the words he can think of that are related to the topic, describe a character, etc.

NOW LOOK WHAT YOU'VE DONE!

You can use this strategy as an assessment tool and differentiate your instruction according to the results. For example, analyze what the students have been able to complete on the reproducible and then use the data to form readiness groups for instruction. Those students whose answers indicate they don't know much about the topic will need some direct instruction; students who appear to know quite a bit about the topic already might benefit from a more in-depth or complex project related to the content.

You might also want to vary the levels of questions you ask, based on what you've learned in this assessment. Some students might brainstorm basic math terms while more advanced students might be challenged to brainstorm all the places outside of school where they might see decimal points.

Reproducible

Chapter Three, Strategy #2

Brainstorming A–Z

Name: Michael
Subject: geometry

A	angle	N	
B		O	oval
C	circle	P	pentagon
D		Q	
E		R	rectangle
F		S	square
G		T	triangle
H	hexagon	U	
I		V	
J		W	
K		X	
L	line	Y	
M		Z	

128

Jigsaw

Jigsaw is a cooperative learning structure (Aronson 1978; Slavin 1994; Kagan 1994, 1998) that can be used in any content area and with any grade level. It helps students to explore material in a relatively short amount of time, and it also builds in both individual and group accountability.

STEP BY STEP

- Have students break into base groups of four students.
- Ask the students in each group to count off.
- Have the number four students meet with other number fours, number threes meet with other number threes, etc., to form expert groups.

BASE GROUP   **EXPERT GROUP**

1	2		1	1
3	4		1	1

1	2		2	2
3	4		2	2

1	2		3	3
3	4		3	3

1	2		4	4
3	4		4	4

OPTIONS

You can differentiate this strategy in a couple of different ways:

- Differentiate according to level of readiness for the content. For example, in a unit of study on states and capitals, take students for whom the content is difficult and ask them to list states and capitals in their expert group. Ask another expert group to design a travel brochure for a particular state capital, and yet another to compare and contrast two states and their capitals. When students return to their base groups, each student can share with the others what was done in his expert group.

- Differentiate the end products. Let the base groups choose, based on their learning preferences or intelligences, how they'll show you what they've done. For example, when studying careers, one group member might choose to perform silent pantomimes of various jobs, one might make a pie graph of currently popular jobs, another might choose to write and then read to the others descriptions of various jobs, and another might choose to create logos depicting different careers.

- The job of each expert group is to study a particular area of the content and then meet back with their base groups to teach that content to the base groups. Let's say students are studying a particular state: Florida. You'd assign each expert group a particular topic—maybe one would study the climate, and others would study the resources, history, and/or geography of Florida. After the expert group on climate meets together, the members return to their base groups to teach the other students about the climate of Florida.

NOW LOOK WHAT YOU'VE DONE!

This activity has all sorts of benefits in terms of differentiated instruction. If you require a student to turn in a report, you're allowing for individual assessment. If you require each *group* to turn in a report or take a quiz on the material, you establish group accountability.

The process fosters shared responsibility for learning. And when the students return to their base groups, those students for whom the content is a challenge will not only have the chance to participate in the group discussion but will also benefit from the dialogue with the more advanced learners in the group.

Numbered Heads Together

Like the Jigsaw strategy, Numbered Heads Together is appropriate for multiple content areas and grade levels. It's also a great way to review because it holds each group member accountable for the learning (Kagan 1994, 1998).

STEP BY STEP

• Put students in groups of four.

• Have students count off in each group so that every group has a number 1, number 2, number 3, and number 4.

• Pose a question or raise an issue for discussion. Have each group put their heads together (not literally; you don't want to spread head lice!) and brainstorm the question or issue you've posed. Explain that they should discuss the possibilities and come to an agreement. Be sure to give very specific directions for this step. Say something like, "Put your heads together and make sure everybody in your group knows [the main theme of the novel or all the ways to make the number 65] and can give evidence to support the answer."

• Give the groups time to work together to formulate their responses and to make sure that each group member will be able to respond successfully if called upon.

• Tell the class that when you call out a number, then within each group, the student with that number should stand.

• Use a spinner or other means to pick a number; call out that number. Let's say it's four.

• The number four student from every group stands.

• You call on any of those standing to respond, or ask for a choral response if that's appropriate.

NOW LOOK WHAT YOU'VE DONE!

You have both "hogs" and "logs" in your classroom, and this cooperative learning structure can meet the learning needs of both groups. The hog is given the opportunity to teach others in the group, but the log can't check out of the activity and go to space camp because she never knows when her number will be called. And the log should be successful in responding because you've told the students to make sure everyone knows the group's answer.

Role Cards for Expository Text

This strategy promotes active discussion by using role cards, and uses colors to differentiate for different skill levels. The example assumes that you're using blue for the less able and green for the more able students.

STEP BY STEP

- Before class, make enough copies of the reproducibles on pages 130–31 so that every student in your class can have one card that's appropriate for her readiness level. Each page contains two sets of cards, so if you have four groups that need blue role cards, you'll need to make two copies of page 130. Cut the sheets into individual cards and then laminate them.

- Also make one enlarged copy of the reproducible on page 129 (Pointer/Signal Words) and post it in the classroom for student reference.

- Divide students into homogeneous groups of four and give each student in each group one of the individual cards from the reproducibles.

- Tell students to read their cards to find out what their roles will be for the group discussions.

- Have them read the book.

- Give students time for group discussion. This is the point at which each member participates based on the role on his card.

- Give each group a large sheet of bulletin-board paper and some markers.

- Ask each group to figure out a way to show the key elements of their discussion by making a graphic representation on the bulletin-board paper.

- Have each group share their graphic representation with the entire class.

NOW LOOK WHAT YOU'VE DONE!

You've given students an incentive to participate, and you've differentiated according to abilities.

Discussion Cards for Narrative Text

Now you're ready to add one *more* level of complexity to the role cards.

STEP BY STEP

- Before class, make enough copies of the reproducible on page 132 so that every student in your class can have one discussion card. These do not need to be color coded.

- Cut the sheets into individual cards and then laminate them.

- Also ahead of time, write specific questions for students on blue (for less able students) and green (for more able students) strips of paper. For examples, see the following page.

- In class, divide students into homogeneous groups of four. Give each student in each group one of the individual discussion cards and one or two of the question strips. Explain that she needs

to answer the questions on the strips and discuss them with her group, based on the role card she's received.

- Have everyone read the book.

- Give students time for group discussions. This is the point at which each member participates based on the topic given on his card.

NOW LOOK WHAT YOU'VE DONE!

By assigning different roles, you're teaching to each student's strengths. You're also inviting each student to become engaged in learning, because everyone knows she has a specific responsibility.

SAMPLE BLUE QUESTIONS FOR NARRATIVE TEXT

Characters

- Who were the main characters? Were they believable?

- Explain how a character in this book reminds you of a character in another book.

Setting

- What was the setting? Why do you think the author chose this setting?

- Read a passage to the group that tells something about the setting.

- Can you think of a place that reminds you of this setting or another story you've read that had a setting similar to this one? Give an example.

Theme

- What is the theme of the story?

- Have you read another story with a similar theme? Give an example.

Resolution

- What was the problem in this story and how was it solved?

- Give two examples of events that contributed to the problem in the story.

SAMPLE GREEN QUESTIONS FOR NARRATIVE TEXT

Characters

- Which character would you like to spend a day with and why?

- Think of a situation that involved the main character and discuss how you might have handled it differently.

Setting

- Think of another setting for the story. How would the story be different if it had taken place in the new setting?

- Why do you think the author chose this setting?

Theme

- How did you learn what the theme was? Give specific examples.

- Give an example of other stories that have the same theme as this one. Did the author of each story use a different technique to present the theme? Give examples.

Resolution

- Can the resolution of this story be transferred to situations in everyday life? Give examples.

- Was the solution to the problem one that you would have selected? Why or why not?

Think-Tac-Toe

This is a great anchor activity to assign to individual students. It allows them to engage in meaningful work while you're involved with other students in a small group.

STEP BY STEP

- Make a copy of the Think-Tac-Toe grid (see reproducible on page 133).

- Identify nine activities related to content that the class is studying. Make some of the activities more difficult than others.

- Write each activity in one of the squares in the Think-Tac-Toe grid.

- Make one copy of the completed grid for each student.

- Explain to the class that each student is to choose one assignment from each line in order to complete a Think-Tac-Toe. Specify how long they have to finish these assignments.

VARIATIONS

Use any of the reproducibles on pages 134–36 as variations on the Think-Tac-Toe theme.

NOW LOOK WHAT YOU'VE DONE!

You have all sorts of opportunities for differentiating with a Think-Tac-Toe grid. You can give students choices that appeal to different learning styles, different intelligences, or different skill levels. This is exactly what differentiated instruction is all about!

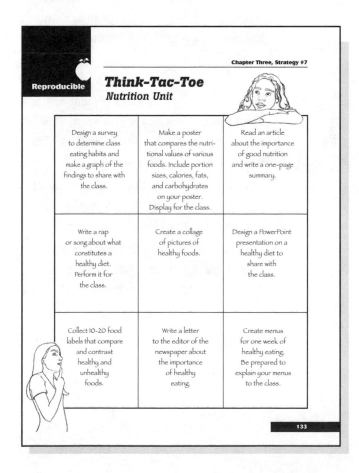

Chapter Three, Strategy #7

Reproducible

Think-Tac-Toe
Nutrition Unit

Design a survey to determine class eating habits and make a graph of the findings to share with the class.	Make a poster that compares the nutritional values of various foods. Include portion sizes, calories, fats, and carbohydrates on your poster. Display for the class.	Read an article about the importance of good nutrition and write a one-page summary.
Write a rap or song about what constitutes a healthy diet. Perform it for the class.	Create a collage of pictures of healthy foods.	Design a PowerPoint presentation on a healthy diet to share with the class.
Collect 10-20 food labels that compare and contrast healthy and unhealthy foods.	Write a letter to the editor of the newspaper about the importance of healthy eating.	Create menus for one week of healthy eating. Be prepared to explain your menus to the class.

133

4-6-8

The 4-6-8 chart lets you and your class invest ten to fifteen minutes up front to create a framework you can use all year long.

STEP BY STEP

- Work with your entire class to construct a 4-6-8 chart that will be posted in the room. If you like, you can start with an enlarged copy of the reproducible on page 137.

- For the first column, "Characters," work with students to list four different characters from any books they've read. The characters don't all have to be from the same book.

- For the second column, "Settings," work with students to list six different settings where a story could take place.

- For the third column, "Events," work with students to list eight different events that could occur in a story.

- Laminate the completed poster and hang it in the room.

- Circle a character, a setting, and an event, and have the students compose a story using the circled items.

- Each week, change the circled numbers and have the students compose a new story using the circled elements.

VARIATION

Ask certain students to create their own 4-6-8 charts and work from them.

NOW LOOK WHAT YOU'VE DONE!

Once you've prepared the initial chart with the class, it takes no time at all to prepare each assignment. Just change the circles! In that one initial brainstorming session, you've created 192 possible combinations, and it's likely that virtually every one will allow your students to differentiate themselves according to their individual interests and abilities.

Reproducible

4-6-8

CHARACTERS	SETTINGS	EVENTS
1. Harry Potter	1. in school	1. losing money
2. Hank the Cowdog	2. at the football game	2. getting scared
3. The Alden Children	3. at the beach	3. seeing an old friend
4. Fudge	4. at the movies	4. hanging out with some friends
	5. in the park	5. having a party
	6. at the mall	6. going shopping
		7. running out of money
		8. finding an expensive necklace

137

R.A.F.T.

R.A.F.T. is an acronym that stands for Role, Audience, Format, Topic. The R.A.F.T. format asks students to write from a viewpoint other than their own to an audience other than the teacher and in a format other than answering questions at the end of a story or textbook chapter. By incorporating four ingredients of writing, and also giving students the opportunity to process and manipulate content, this anchor activity can bring fun and creativity into writing in your classroom.

STEP BY STEP

- Explain to students that this activity requires them to think creatively in response to specific writing prompts.
- Model a sample R.A.F.T. activity. For example, for a unit on health, the assignment might be as follows:

R(ole): Heart

A(udience): French fries

F(ormat): Complaint

T(opic): Effects of fat in the diet

In other words, the heart is to write a letter to French fries, complaining about the effect on the body of the fat in the fries.

- Write on the board the outline for another R.A.F.T. assignment, and ask students to complete it on their own. For a science unit on plants, the R.A.F.T. outline might go like this:

R(ole): Plant

A(udience): Rain

F(ormat): Thank you note

T(opic): Rain's role in growth

- To differentiate, try varying the difficulty of the R.A.F.T. assignments, then asking certain students to complete specific R.A.F.T. activities. Or differentiate by children's interests, letting each student choose the R.A.F.T. she wants to complete.

NOW LOOK WHAT YOU'VE DONE!

You've kept students occupied with *meaningful* work, got them thinking, enhanced writing skills, and potentially differentiated according to interests and skills.

POTENTIAL R.A.F.T. ASSIGNMENTS

R(ole)	**A**(udience)	**F**(ormat)	**T**(opic)
Fraction	Decimal	Love letter	Explain their relationship
Presidential candidate	The public	Candidacy speech	Hope for the future
Unemployed factory worker	Friend	Letter	Looking for work
Reporter	Public	Newspaper article	Causes/effects of the current economic situation
Teacher	Students	Outline or timeline	Events leading to current political/economic/school situation

Now It's Your Turn to Reflect on This Chapter

What is your "aha!" or insight or thinking after reading this chapter?

_____

_____

_____

_____

_____

_____

_____

What strategy will you try first?

_____

_____

_____

_____

_____

How and why might you tailor one of the strategies in this chapter to meet the needs of a specific student or students?

Ongoing Assessment Window

For many years of my teaching career, I thought of assessment as the tests that I gave my students every Friday: spelling, vocabulary, reading, math, science, and social studies. My students got very used to the routine in our classroom. They got so used to it that all during the week their favorite question was: "Is this going to be on the Friday test?"

My goal was to get everything graded and in the grade book before I left school on Friday afternoons. I would stay until 6 PM if I had to, just so that I could get away from it all for the entire weekend.

Wow! Hasn't the view of assessment changed! When I was teaching, standard operating procedure was to teach, teach, teach, and then assess. The students weren't really a part of the whole process. They just waited to see what grades they got on their report cards each quarter.

In later years, as a building principal, I looked at lots of the older students' writing

papers and tried to give them feedback. However, I struggled there as well. I knew I needed to be specific, but often would find myself lacking the language that would really help a student grow as a writer.

I remember one time a fifth grader was describing the local weather and wrote, "The thunder banged loudly." I responded with a comment on the paper: "You need to elaborate more." The student then wrote, "The thunder banged loudly again."

Obviously, my attempt at feedback didn't help the student much.

WHAT WE KNOW ABOUT ASSESSMENT

We know now that assessment is much more than the weekly tests. We know that ongoing assessment of our students really should guide and drive our instruction. We also know that before we assess anything for a final grade we need to provide many opportunities for students to demonstrate their skills and knowledge in a variety of formats.

And we know more than that. We recognize that assessment works best when we give students an explanation of what's correct and what's incorrect, along with specific suggestions for growth; when we provide that feedback to them in a timely fashion; when we give students an opportunity to continue working on responses until they succeed; and when students are a part of the assessment process. In other words, we get the best results when we make the goals clear and give students the opportunity to assess themselves.

SOME QUICK DEFINITIONS

That much we know. But then things start to get fuzzy. Does your head start to spin when people toss around the terms assessment, evaluation, and grading? Let's establish some definitions. Assessment involves gathering and reviewing data; evaluation is judging the data; and grading is the reporting system.

Think about it for a minute in a different context. Recently a good friend of mine went to the local supermarket because the pharmacy there was offering very inexpensive health screenings. Her blood was drawn and sent away to a lab. She got back a report that listed her total cholesterol, HDL, LDL, ratios, triglycerides, and glucose. She took the report to her doctor, who recommended specific treatment to lower her cholesterol levels.

What happened? The pharmacy staff gathered the data when they drew the blood; that was the assessment. The doctor added to that assessment when he asked my friend questions about her family history and her own health. He evaluated the data when he took all the information and began to judge it. He determined that she had high cholesterol, for which he prescribed a course of treatment. Although he didn't give my friend a formal grade, he did tell her that if he had, she wouldn't have passed his "cholesterol class"!

However, the doctor's assessment and evaluation led to an intervention (medication) so that my friend wouldn't fail "cholesterol class." He didn't wait until the end to intervene; he was proactive. In our classrooms, our assessment and evaluation must also drive our instruction so that, if necessary, we can intervene to help each student reach success.

A good assessment program in your classroom should include a variety of classroom assessments. You probably already use the traditional assessment vehicles of pop quizzes, teacher-made tests, and tests you get from publishers. I'm not suggesting that you throw those out but rather that you supplement them with some other ways of observing, gathering, and evaluating student work.

A MANAGEMENT TIP

Have students create business cards so they can share with the class their expertise in both academic and non-academic tasks. Ask each student to identify his own strength in areas such as math, vocabulary, and reading, then design a business card for himself on an index card. One student might be the math expert in multiplication and division facts; another might be the expert in organizing the equipment for physical education. The business cards can be posted in a photo album or on the wall. When students need help, they can consult the "resident expert" for the appropriate topic.

WHAT DOES THIS HAVE TO DO WITH DIFFERENTIATING INSTRUCTION ANYWAY?

Ongoing assessment is at the heart of a differentiated classroom. It's very purposeful. It means that your assessment of your individual students' readiness, interests, and ways of learning, as well as your understanding of their thoughts and feelings, is always driving the decisions you make about your instruction. Throughout the learning cycle, you're constantly gathering and reviewing data and making judgments about where your instruction should go; that's how you help students grow and achieve success. Grading is the final step, the one that takes place after instruction is over.

Can ongoing assessment help your students to succeed? You bet!

Of course, ongoing assessment means you need to be assessing where students are before, during, and after instruction. Each of those phases has its own requirements, so it helps if you think of yourself as an assessor in three areas:

- Determining students' prior understanding and readiness for content as well as what interests them concerning the content. (That's the pre-assessment.)

- Tracking students' progress throughout the learning process as well as giving them the opportunity to track their own growth. (That's the formative assessment.)

- Making sure they've reached the goals that have been set. (That's the summative assessment.)

In this chapter you'll find a variety of options for pre-assessment, formative assessment, and summative assessment to use in your whole-group setting. Keep in mind, though, that assessment is only a first step.

BEGIN AT THE BEGINNING

Turn to pages 138–40 to find reproducibles for a student interest survey, an informal rating scale to help you and your students discover their multiple intelligences, and a learning contract for those students who seem to know the content at a fairly high level already. You might want to use the contract if pre-assessments show that a student needs to participate only in parts or maybe none of the instruction.

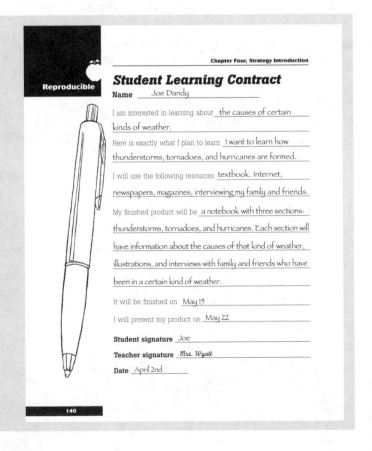

WHAT YOU DO WITH THAT DATA IS CRITICAL

Once you've collected it, you need to examine the data and identify the learning differences and similarities in your classroom. Based on what you learn, you need to make decisions about what your instruction will look like. How will you plan instruction for those students who need something different? What about the students who are ready to move on?

In other words, don't bother to pre-assess if you're not going to do something with the data you collect. You wouldn't want your doctor to read the report on your cholesterol levels and say, "Oh, that's not good. Her cholesterol is up to 310. Guess I'd better file that!"

Timing matters, too. Especially in the beginning, you'll need to gather your pre-assessment data early enough so that you can plan your instruction according to what you learn in your assessments. At times, you may need to adjust your instruction in a couple of ways—for the students who have mastered the content already and for those who will need different types of support to reach that point. Don't let that scare you off. Just make sure you do your assessment early enough so that you leave yourself time to adjust your teaching.

When you get to the formative assessments, timing still matters, but at this point the issue is more one of whether you need to do some reteaching or to adjust the pacing of the instruction—slowing things down or accelerating your teaching. You'll also need to think about when you'll gather additional data (formative assessments) and on which students or groups of students.

Formative assessment is a big part of differentiating instruction in a whole-group setting, in part because these types of assessments can help you celebrate and honor the diversity in your whole group. As you gather this important data, you'll start to see:

- what entry points into content might be effective for certain students
- how best to group students
- how the students are feeling about their own progress
- how to help students set goals
- what mini-lessons you might need to teach to help all students be successful

This is very different from the teach-teach-teach-test approach!

The more you move toward authentic and performance-based assessment, the

A WORD OF CAUTION

Many times teachers will say, "I can't give choices because some tasks are just easier than others or more fun." A fifth-grade teacher told me that one time she gave her students choices of how they would do a book report and most chose a poster. My response is that that's okay; what you want to do is hold all your students to the criteria you've established.

In other words, students are graded on how well they incorporate what you've asked them to incorporate. You offer lots of ways for students to show you what they've learned, but you give them very specific criteria regarding what they'll be accountable for. This is a different way of thinking about assessment.

more you can differentiate and the more choices you can give your students. Choice motivates students and helps them become partners in the learning that takes place in your classroom.

Human Continuum

Like the five strategies that follow, the Human Continuum is a pre-assessment that lets you find out your students' initial level of knowledge, skills, interests, and attitudes. This information will help you plan your instruction at the most appropriate level for each student.

In addition, your students will be motivated and involved as they become partners in the learning process. They'll gain a better sense of what they already know as well as a clearer idea of what they need to know. Use this strategy to supplement ones you might already be using—quizzes, questions, observation, etc.—in pre-assessing your students.

STEP BY STEP

- Place cards at the front of your classroom (perhaps along the top of the chalkboard) labeled along a continuum as follows:

    ✓ I know this!

    ✓ I know something about this!

    ✓ I don't know much about this!

- On the floor in front of the cards, make a line with masking tape.

- Ask students to stand on the masking tape, positioning themselves so each student is near the card that best describes his understanding of the content.

- Ask each student to turn to a neighbor and discuss what she knows about the topic and/or why she chose to stand where she did. Or have students share with the whole class.

VARIATION

For an interesting twist, ask students to fold the line in half and then ask each child to share with the person standing opposite him. This means that those who don't know much about the topic end up facing those who think they know quite a bit. You may find that this leads to an interesting discussion!

NOW LOOK WHAT YOU'VE DONE!

With this quick and simple activity, you've already pre-assessed the students, helped them learn how to assess themselves, and developed a basis for differentiating your instruction of this subject.

Analogies

Analogies are a great way to pre-assess what your students know about content in a fun way.

STEP BY STEP

• Think of ways students can compare the extent of their knowledge to things they already can conceptualize.

• Say you use felines. Ask students what the smallest feline is and they will most likely respond, "kitten." A medium-sized feline is a cat. A large feline would be a lion. Choose comparisons that don't imply judgment.

• Tell students that some of them might be kittens when it comes to what they know about this particular content. That means they really don't know much about the topic yet. A cat would know some things about the topic, and a lion would know a lot about it.

• Tell students you're going to play some music. When the music starts they are to get up and greet other classmates. Those students who don't know much about the topic are to say, "Hi, I'm [student says his name], and I'm a kitten." Students who feel they know a little about the content would say, "Hi, I'm [name] and I'm a cat." Students who feel they know a lot about the content could say, "Hi, I'm [name] and I'm a lion." This gives students

a chance to get up out of their seats and move about the classroom.

ANALOGY CHOICES

You can use lots of different analogies with this strategy. Maybe these possibilities will get you started.

Temperature: cold, warm, hot
Plants: seedling, sprout, full bloom
Humans: infant, child, adult
Sizes: small, medium, large
Weather: rainy, cloudy, sunny

• Give students about one minute to do this, and then have them return to their seats. Stop the music and ask for a show of hands to find out how many students have placed themselves in each category. For example, say, "How many kittens are here today?" This will give you a sense of how much prior knowledge they have.

• Ask those who describe themselves as lions to share something they know about the content.

NOW LOOK WHAT YOU'VE DONE!

This quick activity lets you activate and build on students' prior knowledge. It also demonstrates to the "lions" that you will be holding them accountable for the way they introduce themselves.

Five-Finger Reading Gauge

This pre-assessment empowers your students to select reading material at an appropriate level and gets them involved in their own pre-assessment.

TIPS FOR GIVING DIRECTIONS

You give your students directions every day. But do they often look at you like you're an alien? Try these quick tips for making sure they're understanding what it is you're asking them to do.

- Never assume that your students know what to do just because you've given them directions. Always check for their understanding. One way to do this is to ask them to turn to a neighbor and give the directions in their own words.

- Phrase questions about directions or procedures in ways that elicit specific student responses. Instead of saying, "Does everyone have a book?" say "Raise your hand if you need a book."

- Talk directly to those students who are being asked to do something: "Those at table #1, go to the front of the room."

STEP BY STEP

- Have each student select a book to read and open it to the middle.

- Instruct each student to begin reading the page. Add that each time she encounters an unknown word, she should put down a finger.

- Explain that if the thumb or at least one finger is still up at the end of the page, the book is at an appropriate level of difficulty.

NOW LOOK WHAT YOU'VE DONE!

You've given students a do-it-yourself strategy for evaluating the appropriateness of any reading material they choose.

Greet Students the 4-H Way

One of the most powerful things you can do to enhance your instruction is to stand at the door and greet your students by name as they enter the classroom. Greeting them the 4-H way allows you to push that greeting up a notch and get a sense of students' thoughts and feelings before class begins.

STEP BY STEP

- Make a poster by creating an enlarged copy of the reproducible on page 141 and laminating that copy.

- Hang the poster in your classroom for easy student reference.

- Teach your students that when they come into the room they can choose to have you greet them in any of the ways listed on the poster: a handshake, a hug, a high five, or "How would you like to be greeted?"

- How do they let you know their preferences? A student might simply extend his hand if he wants a handshake or perhaps just say, "I want to shake hands today." Suppose the student says and does nothing. Then you just say something like, "Good morning, [name]. I'm so glad to see you. How about a high five?"

NOW LOOK WHAT YOU'VE DONE!

By using this method, you can pre-assess your students' thoughts and feelings about class. Those who don't respond may need a minute or two of personalized attention from you. In other words, you can figure out from their reactions which students may be having problems at home or a bad start to the morning, so you can give them some extra attention up front and get their focus back on school.

MODELING TIPS

Before turning students loose to work in groups or on an assignment, think through the process or assignment aloud. You might say to students, "I was really confused when I was reading the last sentence in the first paragraph of this text, so I put a question mark on a Post-it note beside the last sentence. But then I kept on reading and in the next paragraph, my confusion was cleared up. So a strategy for me is to keep reading when I am confused because often the author will clear up the confusion for me."

Model directions for students, too. You can show them exactly what it is they're to do either by demonstrating it yourself or by having other students model the process.

Word Toss

This pre-assessment strategy helps students make predictions about text they'll be reading. It also lets you gauge their current knowledge of the content.

STEP BY STEP

- Identify major concepts for the text the students will be reading. Write 7 to 10 words or phrases identifying these concepts on separate pieces of acetate.

- Randomly place the strips of acetate on the overhead so that they appear to have been tossed there.

- Ask students to work in pairs or small groups. Explain that each group should write a sentence or two using some or all of the terms on the overhead. The

sentences should show how the students predict the terms will be related to each other in the material the class is about to read.

- Have students read their sentences/predictions aloud. Don't worry about the accuracy of the statements at this point.

- Have students read the text and check the accuracy of their sentence predictions. Invite them to revise their predictions to reflect what they learned from reading the text.

FOR EXAMPLE

Before reading *The Patchwork Quilt* by Valerie Flournoy, a teacher chose these words for the word toss: *Grandma, Ted, Tanya, Jim, quilt, tells a story,* and *won't forget.* One group of students wrote: "Grandma told Ted to put the quilt on Jim." Another group wrote: "Tanya got in trouble for telling Grandma a story." The students were curious and motivated to see which group got it right. So in a clever way, the teacher had them predict, set purposes, and pre-assess. In that book, as you know, it's the quilt that tells the story.

NOW LOOK WHAT YOU'VE DONE!

By using this strategy, you've given students a chance to practice making predictions and then to go back and evaluate those predictions. You've established prior knowledge. And you've supported reading comprehension by giving the students clues about what they should be watching for in the text.

Anticipation Guide

his strategy helps students anticipate the direction of the text. At the same time, it gives you a chance to pre-assess their knowledge of the content.

STEP BY STEP

• To prepare an Anticipation Guide, identify the major concepts students will be learning in a particular unit of study.

• Craft 3 to 7 statements around the general theme of the material. These statements should be ones that students can agree or disagree with and that will invite discussion. For example, "It's okay to be jealous." Or "If you make the wrong choices, you eventually get whatever you deserve." Or

"Insects are low in fat and make a nutritious snack in some parts of the world."

• List these statements on a work sheet, make copies, and give one copy to each student.

• Instruct students to read each statement and mark whether they agree or disagree with it.

• Accept all answers and invite discussion. This will be the point when you can discover misconceptions or student beliefs that might need some clarification or discussion before studying or reading.

• Read the text or proceed with instruction.

• After they read or study the content, have students review their statements. Give them a chance to change their responses based on what they've read or learned.

NOW LOOK WHAT YOU'VE DONE!

Once again, you've set students up to know what to look for in the content they're about to read or material they're about to study. You've also established an understanding of their prior knowledge of the content.

Anticipation Guide

Conflict is always bad.

Agree   Disagree

_____   _____

There are many different ways to manage conflict.

_____   _____

Most of the time, conflict needs to be avoided.

_____   _____

Signal Cards

This formative assessment strategy, like the four that follow, provides you with options for monitoring student progress and providing feedback during a unit of study. You can also use these strategies to improve and make decisions about your instruction. This approach is especially appealing to students because it incorporates manipulatives in the assessment process.

STEP BY STEP

• Copy the reproducibles on page 142 onto card stock, making enough copies so that each student has a full set. Laminate those cards and give each student a set that includes one card for "Yes," one for "No," and one for "Maybe."

• Explain to students that when you ask a question, you're not looking for them to raise their hands. Instead, you want each child to hold up the appropriate card so you can see if he knows the answer.

• Pose a question about the material you've been studying. Turn to one of those students holding up a "Yes" card and ask her to give the answer. This indicates to students that you're going to hold them accountable for what they say they know.

NOW LOOK WHAT YOU'VE DONE!

You're still working with the whole class. But in just a few minutes, you've assessed all of your students. You've figured out who knows what, or at least who *thinks* they know what. And now you have a basis for differentiating your instruction.

A MANAGEMENT TIP

Work with students to establish rules, responsibilities, and procedures for the classroom. Then practice those things with the students. If a rule for the classroom is "Students come to school ready to learn," discuss with students what that might look like. Maybe the class will decide that students need to come with homework and necessary supplies each day, arrive on time, etc.

Cup It

Here's another approach to a formative assessment that incorporates a different kind of manipulative.

STEP BY STEP

- At a party store, pick up enough stackable plastic cups in assorted colors so that each student can have one red cup, one green cup, and one yellow cup.

- Give each student three cups, one in each color.

- Explain that when you ask a question, each student should stack his collection of cups so that the top color indicates how much he knows about that question. Explain what each color means.

- Ask several questions. Design your questions to get a feel for individual student understanding and for who may need additional help in specific areas.

- For each question, call on someone who has stacked the green cup on top and ask that student to answer the question.

NOW LOOK WHAT YOU'VE DONE!

Once again, you're giving students a chance to assess their own skills and understandings, and you're getting a real quick look at who's all set and who needs your help.

DEFINE YOUR COLORS

Green: The student knows the answer.

Yellow: The student thinks he knows some of the answer.

Red: The student does not know the answer.

If You Know It, Show It!

None of the three versions of this formative assessment requires special materials. Instead, students use their bodies to indicate their level of understanding.

TAKE YOUR CHOICE

- **Stand Up/Sit Down:** Ask students to stand if they know the answer and remain seated if they don't.

- **Thumbs Up/Thumbs Down/Thumbs Sideways:** A thumbs up indicates the student feels he knows a lot about the content; a thumb sideways indicates she knows something about the content; and a thumbs down shows he has little understanding or knowledge of the content.

- **Smiley Face/Sad Face/No Expression:** Ask students to smile at you if they know the content, to look sadly at you if they don't know the content, and to stare at you with no expression if they know something about the content or aren't sure about it. Are you having visions of your students dissolving in giggles? Be sure to model for them the appropriate behavior for this one!

NOW LOOK WHAT YOU'VE DONE!

The first version of this strategy shows you where each student stands in terms of mastering the material. The others offer good variations on that same theme. Kids love using these signals to indicate their understanding.

A MANAGEMENT TIP

Plan carefully how you use your classroom space. If possible, have designated spaces for different activities in the room. For example, set up crates or bins that students can use for turning in work and keeping supplies. Provide individual mailboxes for students; drop in those mailboxes any notes going home, assignments, etc.

Exit Cards

With this formative assessment, students are demonstrating understanding by writing about what they've learned. But that doesn't mean they're just writing a traditional report.

STEP BY STEP

- Give each student an index card.

- Provide students with a prompt or question to be answered as they leave the classroom at the end of the day or the end of the period.

- Use the information on these "exit cards" to inform your instruction the next day. Based on the responses you get on the exit cards, you may decide that you need to have a "coaching clinic" with a small group of students.

FOR EXAMPLE

What might you ask students to respond to on those index cards? Here are some possibilities:

- One thing I learned today was...

- If we got a new student tomorrow, here is what I would tell the student we are learning in....

- Here is how I can use what I learned today.

- Here is how what I'm learning relates to something else I've learned.

- Write down two differences between oceans and lakes and two similarities between oceans and lakes.

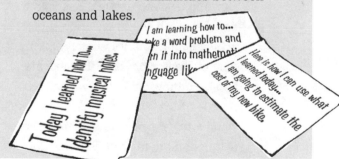

NOW LOOK WHAT YOU'VE DONE!

This strategy gives students a chance to use their writing skills to indicate their understanding of the material. It also gets them reflecting on what they've learned and helps you evaluate in which content areas they're ready to move on and in which ones they need your help.

Student Self-Assessment

Use any of these three strategies to help students in self–assessment and in maintaining their own records of their progress.

TAKE YOUR CHOICE

- **How Am I Doing?** Provide each student with a copy of the reproducible from page 143. Explain that each student is to use that work sheet as a framework for reflecting on and assessing his work at the end of the day or class period.

- **Rubrics:** Rubrics help students understand what is expected and required in learning, as well as what needs to be done to reach the highest levels of achievement. Rubrics work best if this type of assessment is in the students' hands so they can have ownership of their learning. To be sure students understand what's expected, give them copies of an appropriate writing rubric. Go to www.rubistar.com for help in constructing rubrics for your students.

- **Portfolios:** Portfolios are not just a bunch of student work crammed into a folder. Rather, they offer the basis for feedback that students need in order to be involved in assessment. A portfolio is a collection of student work over time. It contains initial samples of efforts such as writing, plus other pieces that are added later to document progress. Often teachers and students collaborate in deciding what needs to be added. Creating a portfolio like this helps students see the progress they make, and it helps you to see how instruction needs to be adjusted to encourage student growth.

NOW LOOK WHAT YOU'VE DONE!

With each of these three strategies, you're making sure students understand what's expected, and then giving them a chance to measure their individual progress along the way. Those are concepts that are at the heart of differentiated instruction.

Three Facts & a Fib

This is a summative assessment. You're used to summative assessments. Those are the things you include at the end of the instructional unit so that you can make decisions about student achievement and the success of the instruction. But this summative assessment is a little different, because it involves finding ways to honor the differences of your learners. It allows for letting your students show you what they know in many different ways.

We so often rely upon the traditional paper-and-pencil fill-in-the-blank, true/false, and multiple-choice questions. But those really reflect only a very narrow range of thinking. In a differentiated classroom, students are active participants, often generating responses that require higher levels of thinking than what's called for in more simple questions. This strategy gives you some options for encouraging more of those student-generated responses.

STEP BY STEP

- Ask each student to write on a piece of paper four statements about any content the class has studied. Three of the statements should be true and one should be false.

- Tell students that each student should move about the room, sharing her list of statements with others.

- Explain that each student should ask his fellow students to try to pick the false statement on his paper.

- Add that if a student fools another student, the one who was fooled should sign the paper of the student who fooled him.

- When all students have examined each other's papers, have them return to their seats.

- Ask each student to count the number of signatures she collected.

- Find out who was able to fool the most students by comparing signature counts.

A FUN INTRODUCTION

To introduce this strategy, try modeling it at the personal level. In other words, make up four statements about yourself—three true and one not. Let each student guess which one is not true of you. Then let each student make up four statements about himself, three true and one not true. Let students see how many people they can fool. This makes a nice get acquainted activity at the beginning of the school year.

NOW LOOK WHAT YOU'VE DONE!

This strategy gives students important experience in narrowing choices. It also provides a great review and helps you to see who "got" what.

Learning Logs & Response Journals

A learning log is a type of student journal that is generally oriented toward subject matter; it's typically used in the content areas to summarize learning, record observations, explain how a problem was solved, list vocabulary terms, or show diagrams or maps.

A response journal consists entirely of a student's writing; in it, the student records personal responses to literature she's reading. The student might reflect on characters, events, or other literary elements of the literature she's exploring.

Learning logs and response journals are both means of helping students understand and manipulate content. You can use either as part of a summative assessment. You can also differentiate them.

STEP BY STEP

- Learning logs and response journals typically involve responses to prompts—but there's no reason every student has to be responding to the same prompt. If the class is studying heroes, you could give some students blue index cards with a prompt that asks, "What purposes do heroes serve?"

- You might give other students yellow index cards with the prompt, "Rank your three greatest heroes and explain your ranking."

- In this way you're differentiating the learning log/response journal assignments according to students' readiness.

SUPPORT YOUR STRUGGLING WRITERS

You can also differentiate learning logs and response journals in a way that supports those students who struggle with writing their responses. All you need to do is invest in a bound composition journal and ask a local office supply store to cut it in half horizontally. This will create little learning logs or response journals, making them less overwhelming for your students.

NOW LOOK WHAT YOU'VE DONE!

This is a great example of differentiation within a whole-group setting. All students are involved in the same activity at the same time, but their specific instructions vary according to their levels of readiness.

Four Square Products

F our Square Products honor the varied learning styles in your classroom while allowing all your students to demonstrate what they've learned.

STEP BY STEP

- Create a menu of ways students can show you what they've learned without relying on paper/pencil responses. Use the reproducible on page 144 as a guide.

- Three of the four squares represent ways students learn: visually, auditorily, and kinesthetically. The fourth square gives options for written products.

- Let students choose from the options listed to show you what they've learned.

NOW LOOK WHAT YOU'VE DONE!

It's important to think beyond the state and national tests to ongoing classroom measures. These can include the traditional formal assessments, observations, and homework as well as more authentic types of assessments such as portfolios, rubrics, stu-

A MANAGEMENT TIP

Hang a yellow highlighter next to the place where students turn in their assignments. Ask each student to highlight her name before turning in her work. This is a great reminder for those students who always forget to put their names on papers!

dent self-evaluations, demonstrations, conferences, learning logs, response journals, and projects. Giving students choices is a key piece of differentiated instruction because it plays to the strengths of individual students, allowing each student to demonstrate understanding of the content in his own way.

Now It's Your Turn to Reflect on This Chapter

What is your "aha!" or insight or thinking after reading this chapter?

_____

_____

_____

_____

_____

_____

_____

_____

What strategy will you try first?

_____

_____

_____

_____

_____

_____

How and why might you tailor one of the strategies in this chapter to meet the needs of a specific student or students?

Chapter 5

Getting Started

Wow! You've finished reading and reflecting on ideas for beginning your journey into differentiation. Just maybe I've given you the courage to begin. Differentiation really is an extension of good teaching, but it does have some complexity to it.

You know how I've been saying that your students will eventually give up if they don't experience some success? Well, you're likely to give up on differentiation if you don't start to experience some success with it where you are comfortable—in your whole-group setting. I hope you can see some clear windows of opportunity to begin to work differentiation into your classroom, and to help your individual students, even while you're still teaching in a whole-group setting.

Change is hard—any kind of change, whether you perceive it to be a good change or a bad change. I remember a time when I was leaving one school to open another, new school. I had served as principal at the old school for a number of years. I perceived the opportunity to open the new school as a positive change, but it was still change, and it was difficult to let go of something I was comfortable with in order to try something new. Knowing this, the president of the Parent Teacher Organization made a wall hanging for me. On that wall hanging was a quote that I refer to over and over again when faced with change:

"It is possible to change without improving, but it is impossible to improve without changing."

Hold that thought as you begin the journey into honoring the diversity in your classroom.

LET'S GET GOING!

As you continue to differentiate in your classroom, be sure to:

- acknowledge what you're already doing
- begin with simple strategies that are easy to implement
- build a circle of support with other teachers
- celebrate your successes
- learn from your mistakes
- keep the students first

Reproducibles

Reproducible

Daily Appointment Calendar

Name _____

8:00	_____	4:00	_____
9:00	_____	5:00	_____
10:00	_____	6:00	_____
11:00	_____	7:00	_____
12:00	_____	8:00	_____
1:00	_____	9:00	_____
2:00	_____	10:00	_____
3:00	_____	11:00	_____

Reproducible

The Parking Lot

Name _____

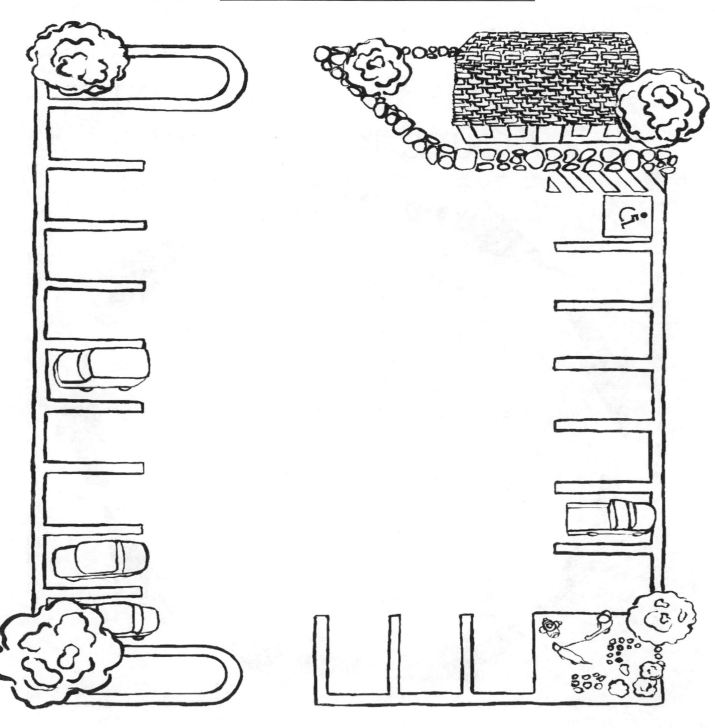

Geometric Questions

Name _____

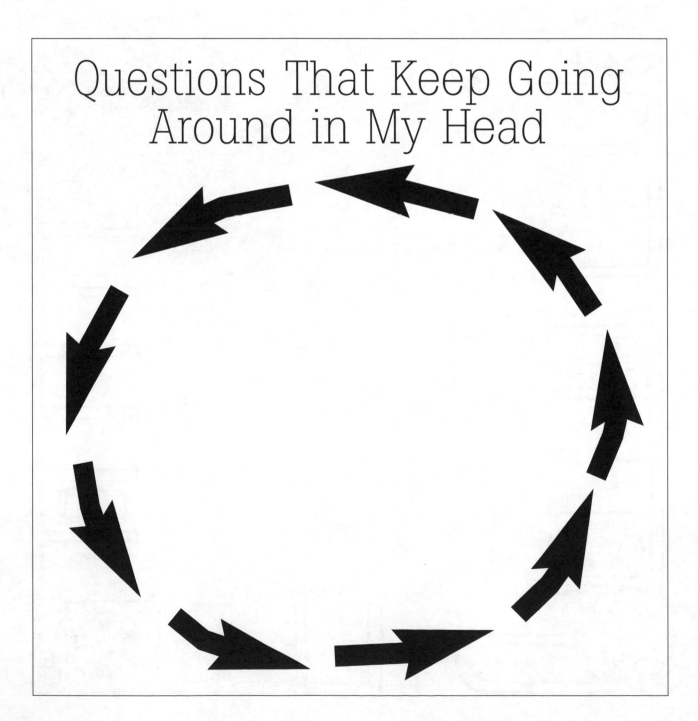

Questions That Keep Going Around in My Head

Key Words & Sample Questions from Bloom's Taxonomy

LEVEL 1: KNOWLEDGE.
Recalling basic facts, concepts, and terms

Key Words: Define, describe, label, list, match, memorize, recall, recite, record, select, show, tell, what, when, where, who, why, write

Sample Questions:
- Which one?
- List . . .
- Name the . . .
- When did _____ happen?
- How much?

Example: List the products of the state of Hawaii.

LEVEL 2: COMPREHENSION.
Demonstrating or showing understanding of facts and ideas

Key Words: Classify, compare, contrast, demonstrate, explain, express, infer, locate, outline, paraphrase, restate, review, rewrite, show, summarize

Sample Questions:
- What is the main idea of . . . ?
- Which statements support . . . ?
- Give an example of . . .
- Explain the reasons . . .

Example: Explain the reasons that Pearl Harbor was bombed.

LEVEL 3: APPLICATION.
Applying knowledge to new or unfamiliar situations; using what has been learned

Key Words: Apply, associate, build, calculate, construct, develop, diagram, display, dramatize, draw, illustrate, integrate, interpret, interview, make, model, paint, plan, reformat, research, solve

Sample Questions:
- How would you use . . .
- What examples can you find to . . .
- Tell what would happen if . . .
- Predict what might happen if...

Example: Construct a timeline of the events leading up to the bombing of Pearl Harbor.

LEVEL 4: ANALYSIS.

Examining and breaking information into parts

Key Words: Analyze, categorize, classify, compare, contrast, debate, diagram, discover, distinguish, illustrate, inspect, investigate, question, separate, simplify, solve, study, take apart

Sample Questions:

• How would you classify . . . ?
• How would you categorize . . . ?
• Can you critique . . . ?
• Make a distinction.
• Separate the facts and the opinions.

Example: Compare and contrast the climates of the states of Hawaii and Texas.

LEVEL 5: SYNTHESIS.

Putting information together in new ways; combining content into a pattern that is different

Key Words: Adapt, build, compose, construct, create, design, discuss, form, imagine, invent, make, prepare, produce, transform

Sample Questions:

• Propose an alternative.
• How else would you . . .
• What way would you design . . . ?
• Predict the outcome if . . .
• Write a new ending.

Example: Write a letter to the editor of the Honolulu *Star-Bulletin* elaborating on the reasons why you think that very expensive shops are taking over along the beachfront. Offer solutions to the problem.

LEVEL 6: EVALUATION.

Making judgments about information, evaluating based on a set of criteria

Key Words: Argue, assess, conclude, debate, defend, dispute, estimate, forecast, formulate, interpret, judge, prove, recommend

Sample Questions:

• What is your opinion of . . .
• What choice would you have made?
• Based on your knowledge, how would you explain . . . ?
• Find the errors.
• Rate the . . .

Example: Would you rather live in Hawaii or where you live now?

Give Me Five!

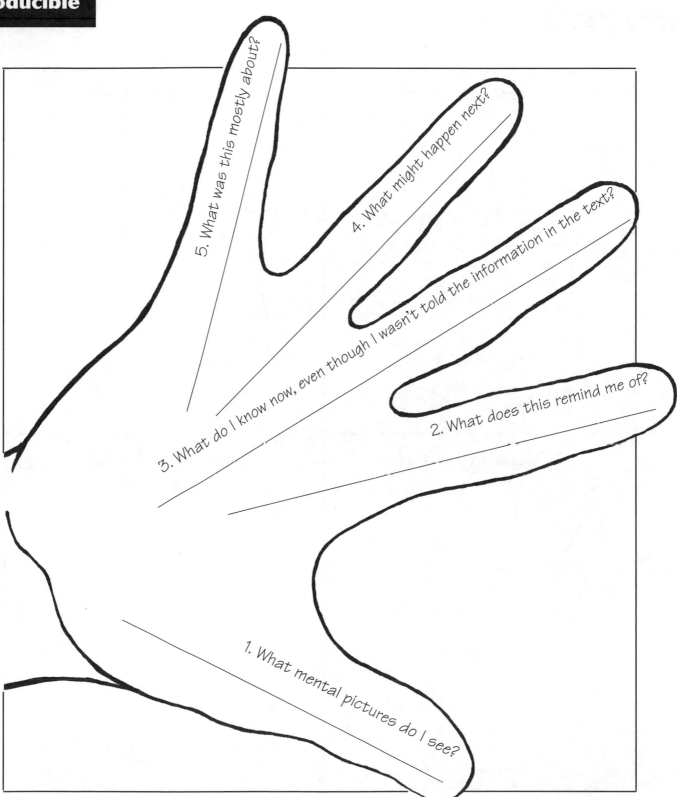

5. What was this mostly about?

4. What might happen next?

3. What do I know now, even though I wasn't told the information in the text?

2. What does this remind me of?

1. What mental pictures do I see?

Reproducible

Give Me Five!

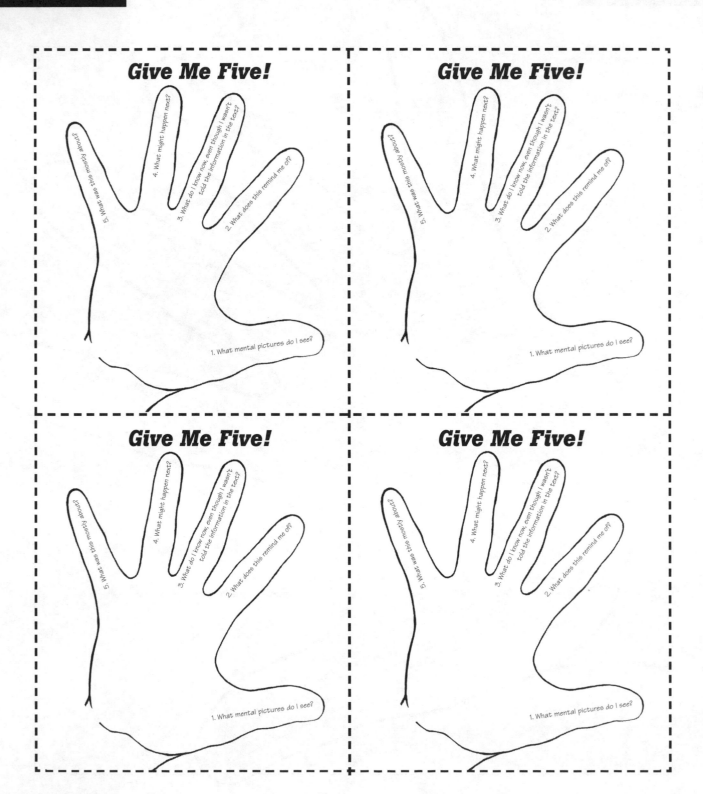

For Visual Learners

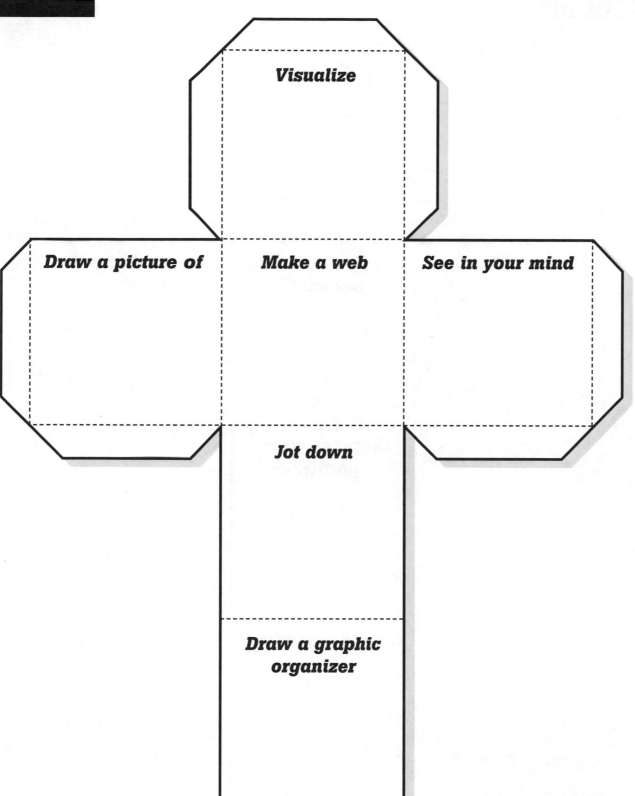

Visualize

Draw a picture of

Make a web

See in your mind

Jot down

Draw a graphic organizer

For Auditory Learners

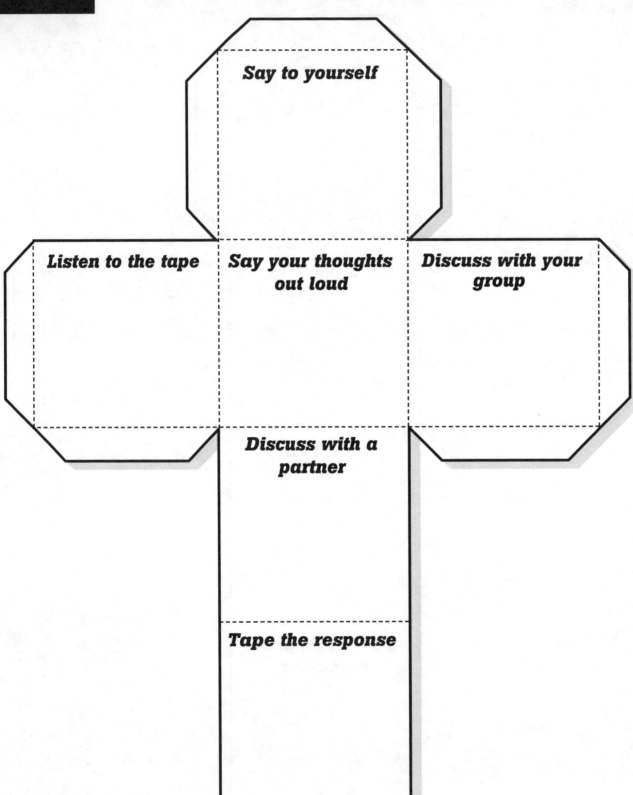

Say to yourself

Listen to the tape

Say your thoughts out loud

Discuss with your group

Discuss with a partner

Tape the response

Reproducible

For Kinesthetic Learners

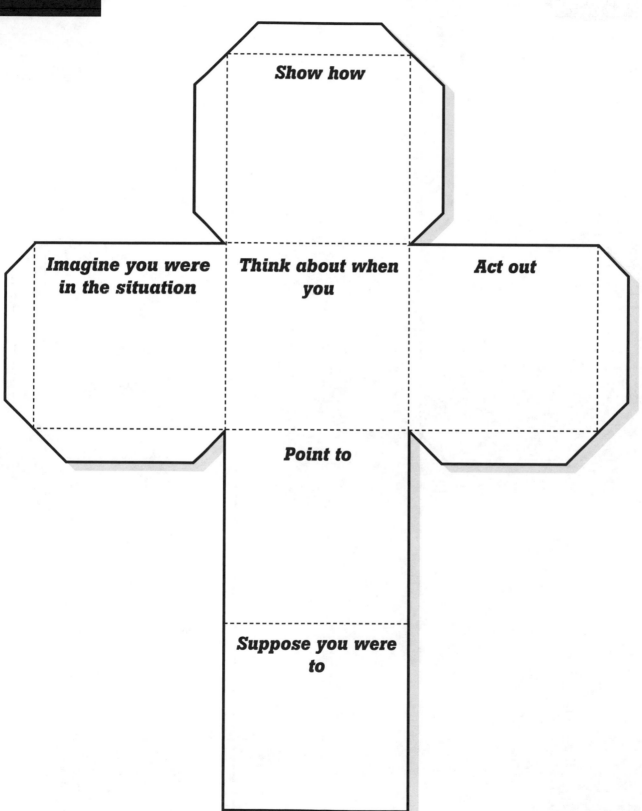

Show how

Imagine you were in the situation

Think about when you

Act out

Point to

Suppose you were to

Cube Pattern

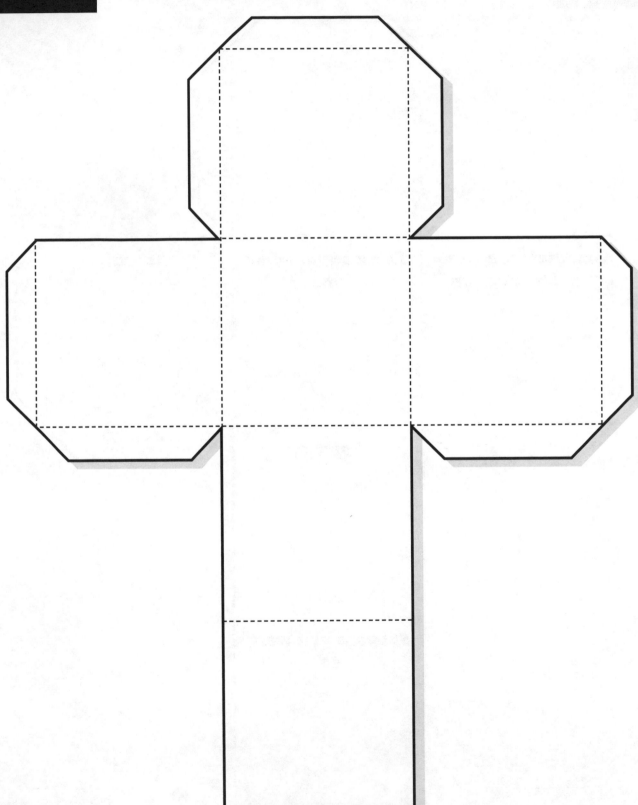

Bloom's Cube

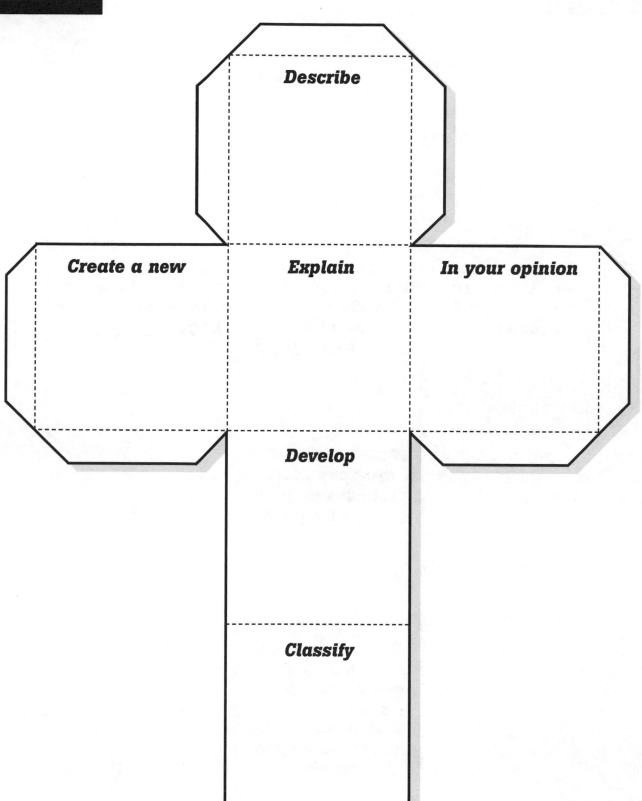

Describe

Create a new   **Explain**   **In your opinion**

Develop

Classify

Math Cube

Describe how you would solve . . .

Imagine what would happen if math didn't exist.

Compare and contrast the four mathematical operations (+ - x ÷)

Formulate a word problem from the number problem on page _____.

Make a game that uses any of the problems on page _____ as a guide.

Diagram or illustrate the solution to the problem on page_____. Write a description of the visual you create.

Comprehension Cube

Describe It

This is how I would describe the issue/topic/problem.

Adapt It

This is how it can be used or how it helps me understand other issues/topics/ problems.

Compare It

It's like _____ and different from_____ .

Argue for/ against It

*I agree with this because_____
or
I disagree with this because_____ .*

Associate It

This issue/topic/problem connects to other issues/topics/problems by making me think of_____ .

Analyze It

This is how I would break the issue/topic/problem into smaller parts or tell what this issue/topic/prob-lem is composed of.

I Have/Who Has?

I Have Who Has	I Have Who Has	I Have Who Has
I Have Who Has	I Have Who Has	I Have Who Has
I Have Who Has	I Have Who Has	I Have Who Has

Question-Answer Relationships

Level I
In-the-Book Questions
Right There

Level II
In-the-Book Questions
Think, Search, and Find

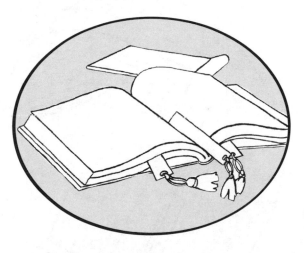

Level III
In-My-Head Questions
Author and Me

Level IV
In-My-Head Questions
On My Own

Q.A.R. Level I Questions

RIGHT THERE

Attributes of Level I Questions

1. The answer is usually contained in one sentence and is easy to find.

2. Often the same words that make up the answer are found in the question.

3. The reader needs only literal thinking to answer the question.

Adapted from the work of Taffy E. Raphael 1982, 1984, 1986.

Q.A.R. Level II Questions

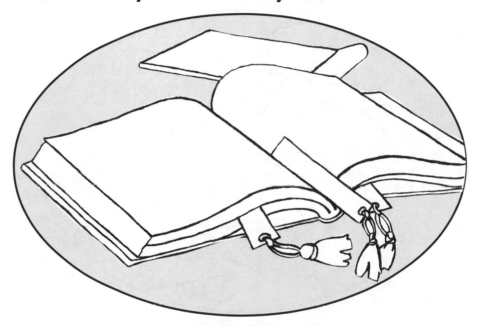

THINK, SEARCH, AND FIND

Putting the Parts Together
Attributes of Level II Questions

1. The answer is found in more than one place. The parts must be put together to answer the question.

2. Certain words—including pointer/signal words, plurals, and conjunctions—indicate that the answer is in more than one place.

3. The words in the question may or may not be the same words used to answer the question.

4. The reader needs only literal thinking to answer the question.

Adapted from the work of Taffy E. Raphael 1982, 1984, 1986.

Q.A.R. Level III Questions

AUTHOR AND ME

Attributes of Level III Questions

1. The reader must read the text to answer the question (text dependent).

2. The reader must use inferential thinking in order to answer the question.

3. The reader relies on prior knowledge and experience.

4. The reader must look for clues and evidence (prove the answer with details).

5. The reader must read *between the lines* as the answer is *not explicit* in the text.

Adapted from the work of Taffy E. Raphael 1982, 1984, 1986.

Q.A.R. Level IV Questions

ON MY OWN

Beyond the Text
Attributes of Level IV Questions

1. The reader need not read the text in order to answer the question.

2. The reader must use inferential thinking.

3. The reader relies on prior knowledge and experiences.

4. The reader must use his own ideas and opinions to answer the questions.

Adapted from the work of Taffy E. Raphael 1982, 1984, 1986.

Reproducible

Question-Tac-Toe

Knowledge *(Write, List, Define, Label)*	**Comprehension** *(Explain, Compare,* *Summarize)*	**Application** *(Apply, Illustrate, Diagram)*
Analysis *(Analyze, Categorize, Solve)*	**Synthesis** *(Adapt, Compose, Create)*	**Evaluation** *(Judge, Recommend,* *Forecast)*
Comprehension *(Outline)*	**Evaluation** *(Debate)*	**Synthesis** *(Compose)*

Question-Tac-Toe
For Visual Learners

Knowledge (Record)	Comprehension (Locate)	Application (Calculate)
Analysis *(Simplify)*	**Synthesis** *(Imagine)*	**Evaluation** *(Prove)*
Synthesis *(Prepare)*	**Evaluation** *(Assess)*	**Comprehension** *(Rewrite)*

Question-Tac-Toe
For Auditory Learners

Knowledge *(Recite)*	**Comprehension** *(Explain)*	**Application** *(Interpret)*
Analysis *(Debate)*	**Synthesis** *(Create and Discuss)*	**Evaluation** *(Defend)*
Analysis *(Question)*	**Application** *(Interview)*	**Comprehension** *(Express)*

Question-Tac-Toe
For Kinesthetic Learners

Knowledge *(Label)*	Comprehension *(Show)*	Application *(Draw)*
Analysis *(Diagram)*	Synthesis *(Construct)*	Evaluation *(Argue by Acting Out)*
Synthesis *(Make)*	Application *(Paint)*	Comprehension *(Categorize)*

Reproducible

100 T.H.I.N.K. Questions

T (Thoughts/Feelings/Opinion/Point of View)
• How do you feel when no one laughs at your jokes?
• Which day of the week are you the happiest?
• What time of day is your favorite?
• What is your opinion of homework?
• What is your parents' opinion of homework?
• Be a baseball glove for one day. Tell what you do.
• If the number four could talk, what would it say?
• What would your journal say if it could talk?
• Pretend you are the principal. Describe your best day.
• How would you feel if you found out you were the teacher for one day?
• Be a pencil. Tell why you are better than a pen.
• You are (character from a book). What is your best (worst) memory?
• Pretend you are a dog. Who is your best friend?
• You are a trick question in math. What is the question?
• How do you feel when it's your birthday? (Answer from your birthday cake's point of view.)
• Two lockers are having a conversation. What are they saying?
• What would decimals say to fractions?
• You are the dumpster in an apartment complex. What surprises do you get every day?
• Do you ever feel sad when you laugh?
• Do you ever feel happy when you cry?

H (How Come?)
• How come the word "concentrate" is on an orange juice can?
• How come you recite at a school play and play at a music recital?
• How come a toaster has a setting that burns the toast?
• How come pushing the elevator button over and over again doesn't make it go faster?
• How come giraffes have spots but kangaroos don't?
• How come students don't have lunch duty?
• How come teachers send home papers with red marks and not yellow marks?
• How come you get in trouble for "talking back" to the teacher? Aren't you supposed to do that?
• How come a teacher can tell if a holiday is coming without looking at a calendar?
• How come Pluto is the only one who stands on all four legs if Goofy and Pluto are both dogs?
• How come you fill in a form by filling it out?
• How come there's not an egg in eggplant?
• How come boxing rings are square?
• How come you set your alarm to go off when you really want it to go on?

- How come water boils quickly unless you watch it?
- How come experience is the best teacher?
- How come a dog is a man's best friend?
- How come Barney is purple?
- How come you don't get smarter when you eat Smarties?
- How come a whole bag of light and fluffy marshmallows makes you gain weight?

I (What If?)

- What if the sun didn't exist?
- What if you went to school only on Saturdays?
- What if you lived where the story took place?
- What if computers didn't exist?
- What if your pet could talk?
- What if George Washington were still alive?
- What if all food tasted the same?
- What if there were no classroom rules?
- What if there were no chocolate?
- What if water didn't freeze?
- What if you awoke and you were 7 feet tall?
- What if there were no desks at school?
- What if water had an expiration date?
- What if you had eyes in the back of your head?
- What if you could travel at the speed of light?
- What if you could feel the earth rotating?
- What if you were invisible?
- What if there were no bananas?
- What if Columbus hadn't discovered America?
- What if your tongue were covered in glue?

N (Name and Next)

- Name all the ways you could say "Great!"
- A hurricane has destroyed the trees in your yard. What do you do next?
- Name all the ways you could communicate if you couldn't talk.
- Your dog begins to talk. What do you do next?
- The saying goes, "When in Rome, do as the Romans do." Name all the things you wouldn't do in Rome.
- Name all the things you wouldn't take on a camping trip.
- 1,2,3,5,8,13. . . What comes next?

- You are camping and drop your food in the river. What do you do next to get food?
- You are riding your bicycle and the tire goes flat. What do you do next?
- Name all the ways you can use a book.
- Name all the uses for a paper clip.
- Name all the good things about homework.
- You wake up during the night and smell smoke. What do you do next?
- Name all the ways you can think of to convince your friend to drink a glass of buttermilk.
- Name all the ways to use a toothpick.
- Name all the words you can make from the word "unbelievable."
- Name all the objects you can think of that are green and hard.
- Name all the reasons you can why it might be good to be early to something.
- Name all the questions you can add to this list of T.H.I.N.K. questions.
- Name all the reasons you should be the principal for a day.

K (Kind of Alike and Kind of Different)

- How are a lunch box and a school alike?
- How are you different from your siblings?
- How are a piano and an elephant alike?
- How are a dog and cat alike?
- How are a toothbrush and a comb alike?
- How is running the same as a ruler?
- How are you different from your parents?
- How are a race car and the President alike?
- How are pictures and postcards different?
- How are risk and change alike?
- How is planning your weekend like solving a problem?
- How is gossiping about your friends like writing a story?
- How are an explorer and an artist different?
- How are last week and last month different?
- How are last year and today the same?
- How are school and a bagel alike?
- How are fireworks and candy canes alike?
- How are questions and answers different?
- How is school different from a party?
- How are people and vegetables alike?

Talk with F.R.E.D.

Facts, Reflections, Evaluation, Decisions

FACTS

✓ What scenes or images do you remember?

✓ What bits of conversation?

✓ What facts do you remember?

✓ What other things did you observe?

✓ What facts do you know about_____?

REFLECTIONS

✓ What was your first response to the scenes, etc.?

✓ Were you excited? Frustrated? Sad?

✓ How did you feel when the video was shown or the text was read?

EVALUATION

✓ What were the most significant events?

✓ Was this book or video important to you? Why or why not?

✓ What was your greatest insight, or what was the biggest thing you learned?

✓ What was the most interesting part for you?

DECISIONS

✓ What would you say about this text or video to someone who's not here?

✓ What decisions would you make now that you've read this text or watched this video?

✓ Would you recommend this to another student?

How Well Did We Work Together?

Group name _____

Discuss each statement with your group members, reach agreement, and make a check on the appropriate line.

	NOT MUCH	A LOT
We listened to each other.	_____	_____
We shared the work.	_____	_____
We all participated by giving our ideas.	_____	_____
We encouraged each other by asking questions.	_____	_____

Participation Pizza

Group name   **Date**

Divide the pizza to show how much each member of your group participated.

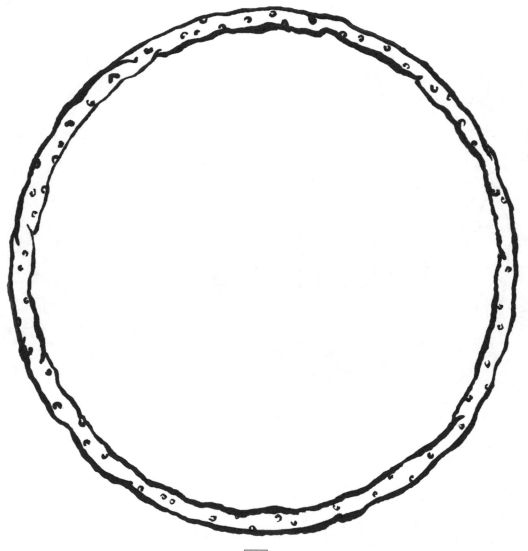

☐ Yes! We met our participation goal.   ☐ No! We plan to improve by _____

_____

_____

_____

Group members' signatures: _____

Group Norms

- Listen to each other.

- Wait your turn to speak.

- Encourage each other.

- Do your personal best.

- Complete the task.

Concept Map

Name _____

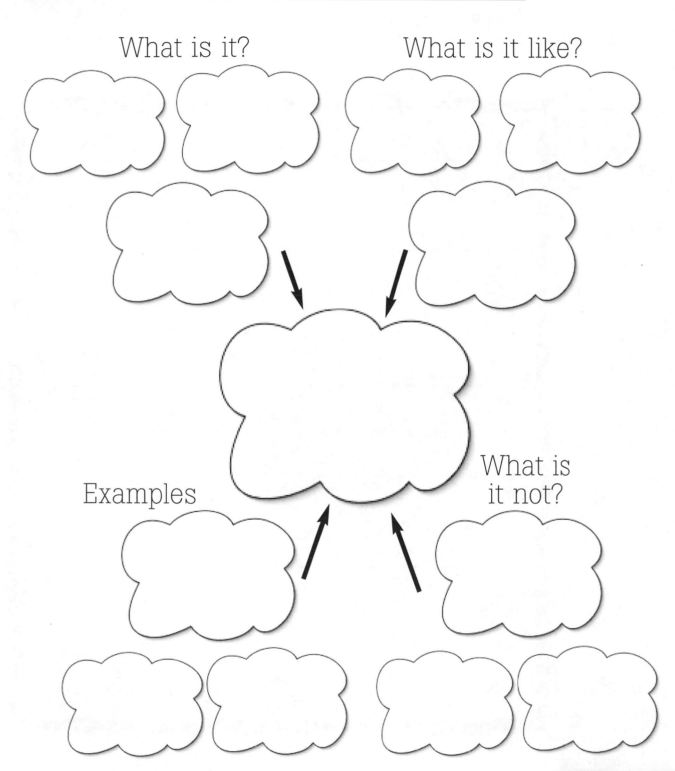

What is it?

What is it like?

Examples

What is
it not?

Brainstorming A–Z

Name _____

Subject _____

A _____	N _____
B _____	O _____
C _____	P _____
D _____	Q _____
E _____	R _____
F _____	S _____
G _____	T _____
H _____	U _____
I _____	V _____
J _____	W _____
K _____	X _____
L _____	Y _____
M _____	Z _____

Pointer/Signal Words

Sequence Text Structure:
first, next, then, finally

Descriptive Text Structure:
for example, to illustrate,
such as, for instance

Problem and Solution Text Structure:
dilemma, problem, puzzle, solved,
the question is

Compare and Contrast Text Structure:
alike, different from, same as,
versus, similar to

Cause and Effect Text Structure:
if . . . then, as a result,
therefore, because

Reproducible

Blue Role Cards for Expository Text

Main Idea Minder
Responsible for telling the main idea of the text

Detail Person
Responsible for giving several details from the text

Key Word Finder
Responsible for identifying key words in the text and being ready to explain to the group what they mean

Question Asker
Responsible for generating a question about the text that can be answered directly by reading the text

Main Idea Minder
Responsible for telling the main idea of the text

Detail Person
Responsible for giving several details from the text

Key Word Finder
Responsible for identifying key words in the text and being ready to explain to the group what they mean

Question Asker
Responsible for generating a question about the text that can be answered directly by reading the text

Green Role Cards for Expository Text

Signal Person
Responsible for identifying signal words and the text structure in which the text is written

Designer
Responsible for drawing a graphic organizer to match the text structure

Graphics Guru
Responsible for discussing how diagrams, charts, etc. help the reader to understand the text

Question Asker
Responsible for generating a question about the text that cannot be answered directly from reading the text

Signal Person
Responsible for identifying signal words and the text structure in which the text is written

Designer
Responsible for drawing a graphic organizer to match the text structure

Graphics Guru
Responsible for discussing how diagrams, charts, etc. help the reader to understand the text

Question Asker
Responsible for generating a question about the text that cannot be answered directly from reading the text

Discussion Cards for Narrative Text

Characters	Setting
Theme	Resolution
Characters	Setting
Theme	Resolution

Think-Tac-Toe

Anything-but-Horizontal Reading-Tac-Toe

For Narrative Text

Directions: Choose three options that do not form a horizontal reading-tac-toe. Circle your choices.

Before Reading	Study the picture on the cover of the book. Make five predictions about the book.	Look through the story and pick out two words you don't know at all, two words you think you know, and two words you know. Share all of these with a partner.	Find a partner and share the reasons you selected your book. Explain what you think it will be about and what you already know about the topic.
During Reading	Use three Post-it notes to mark the text-to-self connections.	Make a map with five circles connected by arrows. As you read, write in the circles the sequence of story events.	Keep a list of the characters as you read. Note each character's name, description, and role in the story.
After Reading	Make a board game about the story. Make sure you include important events in the correct order.	Write a letter to the author letting the author know what you think about the story.	Pretend you are the school librarian. Write an advertisement convincing students to read this story.

Anything-but-Horizontal Reading-Tac-Toe

For Expository Text

Directions: Choose three options that do not form a horizontal reading–tac–toe. Circle your choices.

Before Reading	Look through the text. Find signal words that might indicate the structure of the text. List the words and decide in what structure the text is written.	Look through the text. List the access features (headings, sub-headings, charts, graphs, etc.) that you see.	Pick two subheadings. Change them into questions.
During Reading	Create a graphic organizer that matches the text structure. Use your graphic organizer to take notes while reading the text.	With a partner, take turns reading each paragraph of the text and telling each other what that paragraph was mostly about.	Make a list of words that are unfamiliar to you. Find the definition of each one and write it in your own words. Draw a visual of the word.
After Reading	Write a one-page report telling how narrative and expository text are different.	Write four facts about the text you just read. Make three of the statements true and one not true. See if you can fool other classmates by asking them which one is not true of the text.	Draw a graphic representation of what was important in the text. Use color, pictures, and symbols.

Think-Tac-Toe the MI Way

Responding to Text

Directions: Choose one activity from each line to make a "Think-Tac-Toe."

Write about the main character of your story. Be prepared to present a five-minute report to the class.	In your journal, create a graphic organizer and use it to compare yourself to the main character.	Think of someone you know who is like one of the characters in the book. Write about how they are alike.
Draw a picture of the setting of the story.	Make up a rap about the setting of the story and set it to music.	Build a model of the setting of the story.
Make a timeline to show the major events in the story.	With a group of three other students, create a new ending for the story.	With a group of three other students, create a skit and act out the story.

4-6-8

CHARACTERS	SETTINGS	EVENTS
1.	1.	1.
2.	2.	2.
3.	3.	3.
4.	4.	4.
	5.	5.
	6.	6.
		7.
		8.

Student Interest Survey

Date_____   Name _____

- What is your favorite subject in school? Why?

  _____

- What is your least favorite subject? Why?

  _____

- What do you like to do in your free time?

  _____

- What are some of your favorite books? Why?

  _____

- What past school project was your favorite? Why?

  _____

Rank the following topics according to what you are interested in:
3=very interested; 2=somewhat interested; 1=not interested

_____ Computers	_____ Drama	_____ Writing
_____ Sports	_____ Math	_____ Dance
_____ Music	_____ Science	_____ Reading
_____ Art	_____ Social studies	

- How do you think you learn best? (Examples might be when it is quiet, with a friend, etc.)

  _____

- If you could learn anything this school year, what would you choose to learn about? Why?

  _____

Informal Rating Scale to Discover Intelligences

For each of the following statements, check the characteristics that best describe the student. Note the areas in which each student scores the highest number of checks.

Name _____

Verbal/Linguistic
___ Is highly verbal
___ Has a good memory
___ Writes better than average for age
___ Likes to read and do research
___ Uses accurate spelling
___ Has a good vocabulary for age
___ Enjoys word games
___ Enjoys listening and speaking

Visual/Spatial
___ Likes art class
___ Good at drawing
___ Can visualize things
___ Can read a map well
___ Likes working with models
___ Is good at matching colors
___ Thinks in pictures
___ Can find way in the unfamiliar

Musical
___ Likes music class
___ Hums occasionally during class
___ Likes to listen to music
___ Has a good sense of rhythm
___ Can tap out a beat
___ Makes up tunes
___ Interested in musical instruments
___ Can remember songs

Intrapersonal
___ Likes to be alone
___ Reflective
___ Doesn't give in to peer pressure
___ Likes to ponder and ask questions
___ Can be shy
___ Has sense of right and wrong
___ Interested in personal goals
___ Has an internal locus of control

Logical/Mathematical
___ Likes math
___ Enjoys logic puzzles
___ Likes computers
___ Is organized
___ Can think critically
___ Likes to analyze things
___ Is good at mental math
___ Likes strategy games

Bodily/Kinesthetic
___ Good at sports
___ Prefers to do things and not just watch
___ Uses hands when speaking
___ Likes working with hands
___ Is well coordinated
___ Gets restless if sits too long
___ Catches on quickly to physical skills
___ Looks forward to P.E.

Interpersonal
___ Likes working with a group
___ Likes to be the center of attention
___ Has many friends
___ Likes to organize
___ Good leadership skills
___ A good motivator
___ Wins confidence of others
___ Is sensitive to others' feelings

Naturalist
___ Likes to be outdoors
___ Collects natural objects such as rocks
___ Likes to classify things
___ Often knows names of plants/animals
___ Flexible
___ Enjoys crafts involving nature
___ Keen sense of nature exploration
___ Likes outdoor recreation such as camping

Student Learning Contract

Name _____

I am interested in learning about _____

_____

Here is exactly what I plan to learn _____

_____

I will use the following resources _____

_____

My finished product will be _____

_____

_____

_____

_____

_____

It will be finished on _____

I will present my product on _____

Student signature _____

Teacher signature _____

Date _____

Greetings the 4-H Way

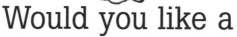

Would you like a

Handshake,

Hug,

High Five,

Or

How would you like to
be greeted?

Signal Cards

YES

NO

MAYBE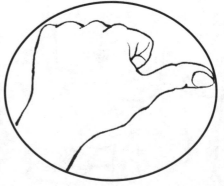

How Am I Doing?

Date_____ Name _____

I met my learning goals today.

I did not completely meet my goals today.

I did not put forth the effort and do my personal best today.

☐ ☐ ☐

Here is what I accomplished.

_____

_____

Here is my plan for tomorrow.

_____

Four Square Products

Visual

Advertisement
Collage
Poster
Flow chart
Venn diagram
Painting
Map
Video
Story map
Timeline

Auditory

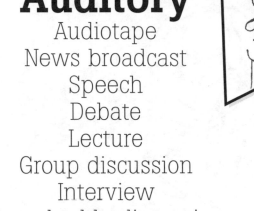

Audiotape
News broadcast
Speech
Debate
Lecture
Group discussion
Interview
Round table discussion
Book review
Teach others

Kinesthetic

A model
Performance of a dance or skit
Sculpture
Mobile
Diorama
Dramatization
Experiment
Pantomime
Role play
Display

Written

Book report
Letter
Poetry
Research paper
Story
Checklist
Journal
Essay
Newsletter
Survey

Recommended Resources

Print Resources

Allen, Janet. *Tools for Teaching Content Literacy.* Portland, ME. Stenhouse Publishers, 2004.

Aronson, Elliot. *The Jigsaw Classroom.* Beverly Hills, CA: Sage Publishers, 1978.

Buehl, Doug. *Classroom Strategies for Interactive Learning.* Newark, DE: International Reading Association, 2001.

Forsten, Char, Jim Grant, and Betty Hollas. *Differentiated Instruction: Different Strategies for Different Learners.* Peterborough, NH: Crystal Springs Books, 2002.

_____. *Differentiating Textbooks: Strategies to Improve Student Comprehension and Motivation.* Peterborough, NH: Crystal Springs Books, 2003.

Gregory, Gayle H. and Carolyn Chapman. *Differentiated Instructional Strategies.* Thousand Oaks, CA: Corwin Press, 2002.

Heacox, Diane. *Differentiated Instruction in the Regular Classroom.* Minneapolis, MN: Free Spirit Press, 2002.

Institute of Cultural Affairs. *Facilitation and Planning Methods.* Phoenix, AZ: 1985.

Jensen, Eric. *Brain Compatible Strategies.* San Diego, CA: The Brain Store, 1998.

_____. *Teaching with the Brain in Mind.* San Diego, CA: The Brain Store, 1998.

Johnson, Nancy. *Active Questioning.* Marion, IL: Pieces of Learning, 1995.

_____. *Questioning Makes the Difference.* Marion, IL: Pieces of Learning, 1990.

Kagan, Miguel, and Spencer Kagan. *Multiple Intelligences: The Complete MI Book.* San Clemente, CA: Kagan Publishing and Professional Development, 1998.

Kagan, Spencer. *Cooperative Learning.* San Clemente, CA: Kagan Publishing and Professional Development, 1994.

_____. *Thinking Questions Smart Card.* San Clemente, CA: Kagan Publishing and Professional Development, 1999.

Kingore, Bertie. *Differentiation: Simplified, Realistic, and Effective.* Austin, TX: Professional Associates Publishing, 2004.

Marzano, Robert J., Jennifer S. Norford, Diane E. Paynter, Debra J. Pickering, and Barbara B. Gaddy. *Classroom Instruction that Works.* Alexandria, VA: Association for Supervision and Curriculum Development, 2001.

Oech, Roger. *A Kick in the Seat of the Pants.* New York, NY: Warner Books, 1986.

_____. *A Whack on the Side of the Head.* New York, NY: Warner Books, 1983.

Pike, Bob. *Creative Training Techniques Handbook.* Minneapolis, MN: Lakewood Books, 1989.

Raphael, Taffy. "Question-Answer Strategy for Children." *The Reading Teacher,* 36, (1982): 303–311.

Slavin, Robert E. *Cooperative Learning: Theory, Research, and Practice.* Boston, MA: Allyn & Bacon, 1994.

Sousa, David. *How the Gifted Brain Learns.* Thousand Oaks, CA: Corwin Press, 2003.

_____. *How the Special Needs Brain Learns.* Thousand Oaks, CA: Corwin Press, 2001.

Tomlinson, Carol Ann. *The Differentiated Classroom: Responding to the Needs of All Learners.* Alexandria, VA: ASCD, 1999.

_____. *How to Differentiate Instruction in Mixed Ability Classrooms.* Alexandria, VA: ASCD, 2001.

Web Sites

www.crystalsprings.com

for books and other products to support differentiated instruction

www.help4teachers.com

for samples of differentiated lessons

www.kaganonline.com

for cooperative learning materials

www.rubistar.com

for help in creating rubrics

www.sde.com

for training and other support in implementing differentiated instruction

Index

Note: Page numbers in *italics* indicate reproducibles to be
used with strategies.

Note: Page numbers in *italics* indicate reproducibles to be used with strategies.

Note: Page numbers in *italics* indicate reproducibles to be
    used with strategies.